UNEMPLOYMENT IN NEW YORK CITY

AN ESTIMATE OF THE NUMBER
UNEMPLOYED IN DECEMBER, 1930, AND
THE SOURCES OF INFORMATION ON
THE EXTENT OF UNEMPLOYMENT
IN NEW YORK CITY

By
EDNA LONIGAN

Published by the
RESEARCH BUREAU
WELFARE COUNCIL OF NEW YORK CITY
151 FIFTH AVENUE
1931

W. C. 32

UNEMPLOYMENT IN NEW YORK CITY

AN ESTIMATE OF THE NUMBER
UNEMPLOYED IN DECEMBER, 1930, AND
THE SOURCES OF INFORMATION ON
THE EXTENT OF UNEMPLOYMENT
IN NEW YORK CITY

By
EDNA LONIGAN

Published by the
RESEARCH BUREAU
WELFARE COUNCIL OF NEW YORK CITY
151 FIFTH AVENUE
1931

W. C. 32

Copyright, 1931
Welfare Council of New York City

THE WELFARE COUNCIL OF NEW YORK CITY

Officers

Honorary President
ROBERT W. DEFOREST

Vice-Presidents
MRS. NICHOLAS F. BRADY JAMES H. POST
HERBERT H. LEHMAN FREDERIC B. PRATT
DWIGHT W. MORROW FELIX M. WARBURG

Secretary
GEORGE J. HECHT

Treasurer
WINTHROP W. ALDRICH

*Chairman,
Executive Committee*
HOMER FOLKS

*Chairman,
Finance Committee*
JAMES H. POST

Executive Director
WILLIAM HODSON

Research Bureau
NEVA R. DEARDORFF, *Director*

Research Committee, 1931

PORTER R. LEE, *Chairman*

BAILEY B. BURRITT RALPH G. HURLIN
ROBERT E. CHADDOCK F. ERNEST JOHNSON
F. STUART CHAPIN MAURICE J. KARPF
STANLEY P. DAVIES WILLFORD I. KING
GODIAS J. DROLET HARRY L. LURIE
LOUIS I. DUBLIN REV. BRYAN J. MCENTEGART
HAVEN EMERSON, M. D. E. B. PATTON
HOMER FOLKS STUART A. RICE
C. LUTHER FRY ARTHUR L. SWIFT, JR.
EDGAR SYDENSTRICKER

PREFACE

When in the late autumn of 1930 it became evident that unemployment of extraordinary proportions would characterize the winter and that special relief measures would be necessary to prevent widespread suffering among the families of the unemployed, the need for more definite information regarding the nature and extent of the disaster became pressing. The Welfare Council and its Coordinating Committee on Unemployment had only the figure of the United States Census for Class A—"persons out of a job, able to work and looking for a job," in April, 1930, as data on the number of persons out of work in the city. This did not include those laid off, who were classified in a separate group. Guessing as to the number of the unemployed was rife.

Since there were some figures on employment in various occupational groups and economic indexes of several kinds, it seemed highly desirable to bring together for the benefit of the social agencies within the Council, and for its Coordinating Committee, all of the data which could throw light on the volume of employment and unemployment this winter.

Accordingly, late in December, 1930, Miss Edna Lonigan, formerly chief statistician of the New York State Department of Labor, was retained to mobilize all of the scattered data as rapidly as possible and to make such estimates as they would permit. In this task, she availed herself of the assistance of many economists and statisticians with specialized knowledge of employment conditions. The Welfare Council is deeply grateful for the generous aid which they extended.

Miss Lonigan has carried through this assignment with the result printed herewith. These findings have been submitted to the Research Committee of the Welfare Council and to other leading economic statisticians of the city who are not on that committee. There has been general agreement among economists and statisticians to whom the findings have been submitted that if Miss Lonigan's estimates err, it is on the side of conservatism. There is reason to think that the number of unemployed persons "usually gainfully employed" in December, 1930, was greater, not less, than Miss Lonigan's estimate.

After Miss Lonigan began her work, the census of unemployed policy holders of the Metropolitan Life Insurance Company in New York City was completed and the U. S. Census Bureau's enumeration of the unemployed in Manhattan, Bronx and Brooklyn was conducted on January 20, 1931. Miss Lonigan has checked her estimate for December against the Metropolitan Life Insurance Company figures in this report. The U. S. Census findings, recently released, show 532,482 persons unemployed and laid off in January in the boroughs of Manhattan, Bronx and Brooklyn. Adding to this figure an estimate for the boroughs of Richmond and Queens gives a total of 609,035 unemployed and laid off in the City of New York in January, 1931. Miss Lonigan's estimate for December was 585,000. Between December and January the index of factory employment declined further and many workers were laid off in retail selling. All of these data are corroborative and substantiate the validity of Miss Lonigan's estimate.

WILLIAM HODSON
Executive Director, Welfare Council
NEVA R. DEARDORFF
Director, Research Bureau

CONTENTS

	PAGE
PREFACE	v
LIST OF TABLES	viii
SUMMARY	1
Two methods of estimating unemployment	1
Data available for estimating unemployment	2
Special employment conditions in New York City	3
ESTIMATE I	5
Population in gainful occupations, 1920	5
Changes in the number of gainfully employed, 1920–1930	6
Census of the unemployed, April, 1930	8
Cyclical unemployment in manufacturing and in non-manufacturing industries	8
Estimated unemployment in December, 1930	10
ESTIMATE II	11
The effect of seasonal changes	11
Employment in factories, 1920–1930	13
The normally unemployed	15
Declining industries and technological unemployment	17
Course of employment in manufacturing compared with other industries	19
Employers' reports from other states	20
Unemployment census of Buffalo	22
Construction	24
Employment in construction, 1929	24
Unemployment in construction, 1930	25
Building contractors	28
Other industries	29
Rate of normal growth, 1920–1929	29
Transportation	29
Trade	33
Public service	36
Professional service	36
Domestic and personal service	38
Clerical occupations	39
Agriculture and forestry	42
All occupations combined	42
SUPPLEMENTARY STUDIES	42
Trend of employment in 1931	42
Loss in wages per week	44
Metropolitan Life Insurance Study	48
Unemployment in Philadelphia and Buffalo	49
Standard Statistics Company	50
Unemployment in 1914–15	50
Unemployment in 1921	53
Method	55

LIST OF TABLES

TABLE	PAGE
1. Two estimates of unemployment in New York City	4
2. Population in gainful occupations in New York City, 1920, similar estimated population, 1929, and estimated number unemployed, December, 1930, by main occupational groups (Estimate II)	5
3. Number gainfully employed in New York City, 1920	6
4. Estimated number gainfully employed in New York City, 1930	7
5. Index numbers of factory employment, New York City	12
6. Wage-earners in manufacturing, New York City	14
7. Estimated number gainfully employed in manufacturing, New York City	15
8. Per cent change in employment and payrolls from October, 1929, to October, 1930	20
9. Index numbers of employment, Illinois	21
10. Index numbers of employment, Wisconsin	22
11. Per cent of full-time, part-time, and no employment, Buffalo, 1929 and 1930—men only	23
12. Per cent of full-time, part-time, and slack work, Buffalo, 1930—men and women	24
13. Estimated number unemployed in New York City, December, 1930, by occupational groups	40
14. Per cent unemployed in certain cities	49
15. Estimate of unemployment, United States	51
16. Per cent unemployed, New York City, 1915	52
17. Estimated unemployment in New York City, 1915	52
18. Per cent change in employment from December, 1913, to December, 1914	53

UNEMPLOYMENT IN NEW YORK CITY

SUMMARY

The information available for estimating the number of unemployed in the United States is very incomplete. The information available for New York City is very much less satisfactory than that for the United States as a whole.

Two Methods of Estimating Unemployment

In order to arrive at as accurate an estimate of unemployment in New York City as possible, two separate methods were used. Both started from the number of gainfully employed persons reported in the Census of Occupations for 1920, that is, the number of people counted by the Census as normally working for pay, including employees, proprietors and those looking for work, and excluding housewives and others who may be producers but receive no money return.

For the first estimate, the proportion of gainfully employed persons in the population was assumed to have remained the same from 1920 to 1930. This assumption gave an estimate of the gainfully employed population in 1930 as 3,163,701. The unemployment for December, 1930, was derived from the Federal Census of Unemployment figures for April, 1930, by estimating the proportion of people to be added to cover those "laid off," whom the Census Bureau had not tabulated, and by estimating, from known figures for manufacturing, how far unemployment for all industries had increased in December compared with April, when the census of unemployment was taken. This method gave 585,000 unemployed.

The second method was much more elaborate. It consisted in breaking down the Census of Occupations for 1920 into its significant groups, and estimating from them the supply of workers available in 1929 and those employed in 1930. The difference was the total number of unemployed. Where it was possible, official figures were secured. Elsewhere data were taken from manufacturers' reports, from union or trade estimates, from corresponding series for other localities, and for series other than employment—such as building contracts, department store sales, etc.—for New York City.

Data Available for Estimating Unemployment

The area of estimate was reduced so far as possible, but for some items no very definite information was at hand. There reliance was had upon qualitative knowledge of industry, upon the more or less well-known relationships of industries to each other, of related movements within various parts of an industry such as building, or retail trade, and especially upon knowledge of the industrial conditions peculiar to New York City. While not the most satisfactory procedure in statistical work, this method is necessarily relied upon constantly in practical enterprises where errors in judgment are paid for by costly mistakes. Its risks can be minimized both by extensive concrete knowledge of industry, by conservatism in the use of varying estimates, and the judgment or weighting-sense used in putting them together.

It must be remembered that arithmetic series wholly accurate in themselves may be misused through the very absence of that qualitative knowledge which determines just what they really mean. An example is the "downward drift" in employment series based on a sample list of employers—emphasized by Dr. William A. Berridge and Mr. Woodlief Thomas—which was due to no error in the compilation of the figures but leads to a very serious error in their interpretation if ignored over a long period of time.

Whatever the hazards of estimating, the second estimate of unemployment made by putting the pieces together came out almost exactly where the first one did, with about 18,000 more people in gainful occupations in 1930 than in Estimate I (a difference of 0.6 per cent). The number of unemployed was estimated by the second method as 572,572. The percentage of unemployment was 18.5 in the first estimate and 18.2 in the second. The actual number in both cases was well over half a million "unemployed and willing to work," as a minimum estimate. This does not include the people released by the department stores after Christmas or by many other establishments at the year-end.

Special Employment Conditions in New York City

In this study three assumptions are made about New York City conditions. It is assumed that there is a large pool of reserve labor in New York City, because of migration, the inequality of wealth, the ease of getting workers, and similar conditions that encourage an uneconomical use of labor by employers, and that make New York more like London than most Americans quite realize. Though these conditions are not so pronounced here, the tendency toward a large labor surplus is very marked.[1]

It is assumed also that if New York City construction and other industries send large numbers of men upstate to work on roads, engineering projects and other work far from any city, these people must return to New York City in the winter. It may often be wise to discourage people from migrating in hard times, but these people are not a charge on the community near which they were last working. Labor like capital must flow to the market and New York City is the biggest market.

It is also assumed that a very high proportion of students have gone from our school system into clerical occupations without any regard for the demand for such labor. At the same time clerical work has been subject to severe technological unemployment through the use of machinery and the economizing in the use of workers. The State Employment Bureau shows a ratio of over nine hundred clerical workers applying for each one hundred clerical jobs, but even a year ago there were over four hundred applicants. This group raises the unemployment figure considerably, and it may be much under-estimated in this report. Only the most conservative figure was taken.

Technological unemployment—the much debated item—was also estimated very conservatively. It was assumed that (1) the manufacturing industries (and clerical work also) continued to exert a strong pull on the new workers coming into the labor market, although they might be letting other workers go, (2) that a large part of the readjustment of workers in expanding industries—of which we expect so much—is absorbed in manufacturing itself, in automobile, radio, and electrical manufactures, and that the net reduction in manufacturing is over and above all these additions, (3) that the workers released from industries where new processes were replacing old skills might have obtained jobs in other industries but that they had to compete with a large volume of new labor coming on the market annually. It is the normal tendency of industry to keep its surplus workers in a reserve pool attached to the industry and to distribute the same employment among a larger

[1] Perhaps it should be mentioned that the prevailing economic theory holds that there is no true surplus of labor, or labor pool, for two reasons, first, that in the long run there can be no surplus of labor unless there is a shortage of land or capital, and second, that labor flows to places where demand is greatest. These generalizations are both true and important, but it is also true that labor can be —and unquestionably is—underemployed when there is a temporary shortage of enterprise, such as exists today, and also when industry undergoes reorganization, which seems to be almost continuous. Labor undoubtedly makes great adjustments through its own mobility, but they are not enough, and labor mobility is, for many reasons, seriously restricted in New York City.

group of people. It is assumed also that technological unemployment, except in clerical and other salaried occupations, was less general in New York City than in the United States as a whole. The pre-existing unemployment traceable to technological changes in manufacturing is not likely, therefore, to be any smaller than the figure given but it may be much larger.

Attention is called also to the fact that wherever unemployment is calculated from the decline in the numbers employed in factories or from any employers' records, allowance must be made for the reserve of employment (apart from technological unemployment) which is never all employed at any one time, because industries and factories do not dovetail in their demands for labor. Maximum figures from employers' records never give the full labor supply. A decline of 20 per cent in **employment** always means **unemployment** of **more** than 20 per cent, to allow for the "normally unemployed."

The conclusion of 18 per cent unemployed among the usually gainfully employed population of New York City in December is

TABLE 1. TWO ESTIMATES OF UNEMPLOYMENT IN NEW YORK CITY

Gainfully employed
- Estimate I—from census of general population
  - April, 1930.................................... 3,118,701
  - Increase April to December, 1930.............. 45,000
  - December, 1930............................... 3,163,701
- Estimate II—by separate industries
  - End of 1929.................................. 3,083,591
  - Increase in 1930............................. 62,100
  - End of 1930.................................. 3,145,691
- Difference...................................... 18,010
- Percentage difference (Estimate I over Estimate II)............ 0.6

Number of unemployed, December, 1930
- Estimate I—from U. S. Census, April, 1930................. 585,000
- " II—itemized by separate industries................... 572,572

Percentage unemployed of all persons in gainful occupations
- Estimate I...................................... 18.5
- " II... 18.2

to be compared with unemployment of those able and willing to work of 16.0 per cent in the Buffalo sample census of November, 1930; with 15 to 18 per cent reported by the Wharton School for Philadelphia in November; with 23.3 per cent among industrial policyholders in New York City in January, 1931 by the Metropolitan Life Insurance Company; and with a 14 per cent decline in an average of 160 series representing trade and industry compiled by the New York Federal Reserve Bank,[1] and including a large amount of agriculture and raw foodstuffs in which there was almost no decline in activity, and which are not characteristic of New York City industries.

Perhaps it is important to remind ourselves that, from the point of view of the worker in need, the immediate results are the same whether unemployment is cyclical or seasonal or "normal" or technological in origin. From the point of view of cause or of control, however, the four types are entirely different, and need radically different kinds of treatment.

TABLE 2. POPULATION IN GAINFUL OCCUPATIONS IN NEW YORK CITY, 1920, SIMILAR ESTIMATED POPULATION, 1929, AND ESTIMATED NUMBER UNEMPLOYED, DECEMBER, 1930, BY MAIN OCCUPATIONAL GROUPS (ESTIMATE II)

Occupational group	Number in gainful occupations[a]		Estimated number unemployed, Dec., 1930
	Census, 1920	Estimated, 1929	
Construction． ． ． ． ． ． ． ． ． ． ． ． ． ． ．	(b)	234,000	62,093
Manufacturing． ． ． ． ． ． ． ． ． ． ． ． ． ．	794,182[c]	776,447	212,195
Transportation． ． ． ． ． ． ． ． ． ． ． ． ．	241,378	285,504	54,944
Trade． ． ． ． ． ． ． ． ． ． ． ． ． ． ． ． ． ． ． ．	392,397	497,393	32,863
Public service． ． ． ． ． ． ． ． ． ． ． ． ． ．	80,875[d]	119,260	1,730[e]
Professional service． ． ． ． ． ． ． ． ． ．	168,037	207,829	14,949
Domestic and personal service． ． ．	306,290	378,059	49,768
Clerical occupations． ． ． ． ． ． ． ． ． ．	382,414[d]	581,244	85,004
Agriculture, forestry and mining．	7,709	3,855	386
Total． ． ． ． ． ． ． ． ． ． ． ． ． ． ． ． ． ． ．	2,531,412[f]	3,083,591	510,472
Net addition to employable population in 1930． ． ． ． ． ． ． ． ． ． ． ． ． ． ．			62,100
Grand total． ． ． ． ． ． ． ． ． ． ． ． ． ． ．			572,572

[a] Including unemployed.
[b] The Census of Occupations does not separate manufacturing and construction.
[c] Derived from the biennial Census of Manufactures, which is compiled on a somewhat different basis from the Census of Occupations. See pp. 23 and 56.
[d] See p. 41, footnote[e].
[e] Increase in number employed.
[f] The total as reported by the Census of Occupations for all nine groups.

ESTIMATE I

Population in Gainful Occupations, 1920

In order to arrive at an estimate of the number of workers unemployed in New York City, it is necessary first to know the number of people employed. The source for this information is the United States Census of Occupations, and the latest tabulated information is that for 1920. Probably the shift in occupations in the United

[1] *Monthly Review of Credit and Business*, New York Federal Reserve Bank, January, 1931, p. 5.

States between 1920 and 1930, however, has been greater than in any decade of our history.

The 1920 Census of Occupations shows the gainfully employed population of New York City distributed in seven principal occupational groups. Manufacturing and mechanical pursuits employed nearly one million workers, mostly men. Those groups include the two important wage-earning industries of manufacturing and construction. Clerical occupations and trade came next, each with about 400,000 workers. Domestic service accounted for about 300,000, and transportation for nearly 250,000. Professional and semi-professional work accounted for about 170,000 and public service for 60,000. Agriculture and mineral production are not important in New York City, but they have their representation. Manufacturing, clerical work, and domestic and personal service account for the bulk of employed women, in the order mentioned.

Changes in the Number of Gainfully Employed, 1920–1930

In applying these 1920 figures to 1930 conditions, it is necessary to consider several difficulties, although for Estimate I we need consider only the number of gainfully employed as a whole. The year 1920, especially in the beginning of the year, when the census was taken, was in the period of extremely high postwar inflation. The cost of living was very high, and in many families more women and young people were working as a result of the war and the cost of living than had previously been gainfully employed. Between 1920 and 1930, we had the deflation of prices in 1921, a fall in the

TABLE 3. NUMBER GAINFULLY EMPLOYED IN NEW YORK CITY, 1920[a]

U. S. Census of Occupations, 1920

Occupational group	Men	Women	Total
Total population	2,802,638	2,817,410	5,620,048
Gainfully employed	1,839,685	691,727	2,531,412
Per cent gainfully employed	65.6	24.6	45.0
Agriculture, forestry, animal husbandry	6,764	345	7,109
Extraction of minerals	575	25	600
Manufacturing and mechanical pursuits	748,183	204,129	952,312
Transportation	218,368	23,010	241,378
Trade	338,298	54,099	392,397
Public service	60,030	845	60,875
Professional service	100,028	68,009	168,037
Domestic and personal service	149,623	156,667	306,290
Clerical occupations	217,816	184,598	402,414

[a] These figures include proprietors, officials and managers, and people temporarily unemployed, who are supposed to report their regular occupation.

cost of living, and the readjustment of war-time employment. Some women were undoubtedly replaced in industry, and we have had an enormous increase in school and college registration.

These factors would tend to reduce the proportion of gainfully employed in the population. On the other hand, we have had a strong tendency for married women to remain in employment in the New York City district, probably an increased tendency for women in general to become self-supporting, probably a slight increase in the proportion of adults in the population, and two other influences the effect of which is even harder to measure.

The decade 1920–1930 was the period in which rationalization—the policy of extreme economy in the use of capital and labor, and the substitution of machinery for labor whenever parts of the industrial process could be made automatic or semi-automatic—has been proceeding at a greatly increased pace. This so-called "technological unemployment" has had the immediate effect of reducing the demand for labor until new industries arise to create new demands. It has not, however, reduced appreciably the wage-earning population. It leaves the same number of people dependent upon an industry, but simply distributes employment unevenly within the group of people attached to the industry.

In the decade from 1920–1930, we have also had a rapid movement of population from the farms to the industrial cities. This affects first the cities where new industries are developing, or those near a large reserve of farm population. But impulses are transmitted rapidly through the industrial system. Cities like Binghamton, Buffalo, and Syracuse are influenced by the labor coming from the farms, and it is not very long before this surplus must be felt in some form in New York City.

For these reasons, therefore, it is likely that the proportion of those dependent upon earned incomes in the population of New York City will not be smaller in 1930 than it was in 1920, and it may well be larger. In the table below, the proportion of "gainfully

TABLE 4. ESTIMATED NUMBER GAINFULLY EMPLOYED IN NEW YORK CITY, 1930

Subject	1920	1930
Total population	5,620,048	6,930,446
Gainfully employed		
Per cent	45.0	45.0 (assumed)
Number	2,531,412	3,118,701 (estimated)

employed" for 1920 has been used unchanged to estimate the number gainfully employed in the population of 1930. The inference is that this estimate is more likely to be too low than too high. But a change in the proportion of newly arrived immigrants of working age and the increase in school and college attendance are the factors that would tend to lower the final figures.

There was a gain of 23.3 per cent in the population of New York City between 1920 and 1930 and, in spite of deep and far-reaching changes in industry, there is no reason to assume that the proportion of the population that works for a money return has declined appreciably. There has probably been, therefore, a gain of at least 23 per cent in the number of the would-be "gainfully employed."

Census of the Unemployed, April, 1930

The U. S. Census, taken on April 1, 1930, included for the first time a count of the unemployed. This count showed 234,854[1] people in New York City who habitually worked but were then "unemployed." The difficulty with this figure is that if a man was "laid off" by a firm, with some prospect of getting his job back, but with no present job and no income, he was not classified as unemployed. How many belonged in the classification "laid off" we do not know. It is probable, however, that "laying off" is more common in smaller cities and those with large plants, where men are more identified with their particular job and the possible range of jobs is smaller than in New York City. Even so, the proportion was large.

Furthermore, April 1 was before the second break in the stock market and before the seriousness of the depression and its probable duration were admitted. We must, therefore, estimate the increase in unemployment between April, 1930, and December, 1930, the date of this report.

Cyclical Unemployment in Manufacturing and in Non-Manufacturing Industries

We may arrive approximately at the relative amount of displacement of workers before and since April 1, 1930, by comparing the displacement in manufacturing for the two periods and estimating how far the movement of unemployment in other industries before and after April 1 corresponded with the movement in manufacturing before and after that date. This is a comparison not of the amplitude but of the timing of the cycle.

The index of factory employment in New York City fell from

[1] Since this report was written, revised figures have been released by the U. S. Bureau of the Census giving 231,099 as the number unemployed, April 1, 1930.

95.6 in October, 1929 to 88.1, the average of March 15 and April 15, 1930 (the nearest equivalent to the census date, April 1, 1930). This is a decline of 7.5 points. From April 1 to December 15, 1930, the same labor market index for New York City fell to 77.0, an additional decline of 11.1 points,[1] or one and one-half times as far in the second period as in the first.

How far can we assume that the known decline of employment in manufacturing in the two periods was typical of the unknown decline in the other industries? For two reasons we have to assume that the decline for all industries, if known, would be greater (in the second period compared with the first) than that for manufacturing. In the first place, employment in manufacturing responds more promptly to cyclical influences than does employment in wholesale or retail trade, service industries, communication, or transportation. The nearer an industry is to the consumer the more slowly it responds to the cycle. The nearer it is to raw materials the more it responds. Manufacturing, therefore, is likely to feel the effects of the business cycle earlier than almost any other industries in New York City. This is not necessarily true for the whole United States. The lag in the non-manufacturing employments in New York City would mean that their downward movement started a little later and gained its full momentum later than did manufacturing. A relatively larger decline, therefore, would take place in the second half of the period than showed for manufacturing.

In the second place, April is a month of quickening activity in all outdoor industries, and December is a month of quiescence in all outdoor industries and in much of the business incidental to Christmas, where the work has to be done well before consumer purchasing is at its height. January alone is worse. Building is the principal outdoor industry in New York City. But again some of the men and women who are employed upstate in building, fruit picking, and road work—not to mention regular farm work—must depend on the big cities to furnish their winter employment, or go without. The country cannot furnish it. Breadlines begin to grow, and municipal lodging houses become full in the late fall and winter, not merely because it is cold but because casual work, in or out of the city, comes to a standstill.

For these reasons, therefore, we must not only assume that the volume of unemployment in manufacturing was more than doubled in the period after April, 1930, but further, that unemployment in the non-manufacturing industries increased at an even more rapid

[1] See Table 5, p. 12.

rate because it started later in many such industries. The one obvious exception is retail trade, where employment should go up for Christmas.

But again a very large proportion of the manufacturing carried on in New York City is for the Christmas trade. If manufacturing in New York City declined as it did in the fall season, which is closely associated with trade, some similar effect must have been visible in trade. Furthermore, for the reasons mentioned below, it is fair to assume that the very encouraging figures on department stores sales in New York City are not typical of the entire situation in retail trade. Of course, stores which move their goods by cutting prices to maintain volume will need sales clerks and delivery men to handle them. But here again price cuts are a reason for the employer to economize on service and a reason why the buyer is willing to take less service.

In spite of the Christmas expansion in retail trade, therefore, we are taking the most conservative estimate possible in assuming that cyclical unemployment in non-manufacturing industries was twice as great after April, 1930, as before, and probably even more than twice as great.

Estimated Unemployment in December, 1930

We must assume, however, that 234,854, the number reported unemployed in the Census of April 1, 1930, includes "normal unemployment," technological unemployment, and cyclical unemployment. Unemployment as indicated by employers' payrolls increased by something over 150 per cent. Unemployment also increased by the closing of the outdoor industries and the seasonal migration in search of city jobs, greatly intensified by the depression. So much of the 234,854 as was technological unemployment did not, of course, increase except as the depression had already caused many employers to study methods of economizing in men and women workers, over and above the cuts in working forces necessitated by reduced business alone. Depressions always have some such effect, and this one is going to lead to more economizing of labor—technological displacement—than other depressions have done.

If we start, therefore, from 234,854 in April, we must first add something for the men "laid off" but not "fired." Preliminary returns from sample states published by the Bureau of the Census indicate that the ratio of "lay-offs" to other unemployed is 30 per cent. Assuming that "lay-offs" are more common outside than in New York City, and taking an estimate that errs on the side of caution, we must add at least 15 per cent to the April Census figures. That gives us an additional 35,000[1] people, or a total in April of at least 270,000. If we raise this figure not by 150 per cent, the ratio for manufacturing, but only by 100 per cent, in spite of the tendency for non-manufacturing industries to make their reductions later in the business cycle, we arrive at an estimate of 540,000 unemployed in December, with every prospect that more people will be out of work in January, and with every indication that the figure should be higher and not lower.

Further allowance must be made for the new workers coming on the labor market from April 1 to the middle of December, eight and one-half months. Given a minimum increase of 2 per cent of the gainfully employed a year, we should have about 45,000. This gives us a total of at least 585,000 people unemployed and willing to work in December, 1930. The estimate of gain in occupied population in 1930 based on the gain in population is net, that is, it is over and above the deaths for the period.

ESTIMATE II

The second method of estimating the number of the unemployed in New York City was to proceed not from the whole but from the separate parts of the gainfully employed population, and by gathering together the available special information about each industry, to derive an estimate of the total unemployment by a method exactly the opposite of that used in Estimate I.

For this second method it is necessary to estimate the number of people in each main occupation in 1930, as well as the proportion unemployed in December. In general it is assumed that 1929 was a year of high employment "under present conditions," that is, disregarding technological unemployment.

The Effect of Seasonal Changes

In using figures from employment and from other series we must observe two important precautions. The percentage decline in manufacturing employment between September, 1929, and September, 1930 is a direct measure of decline because industry was active in September, 1929. In October, 1930, a decline of 15 per cent over the preceding year would still in most series indicate a decline of 15 per cent from a high level. In December, 1929, however, business

[1] Since this report was written, figures have been released by the U. S. Bureau of the Census giving 36,173 as the number counted as "laid off" on April 1, 1930.

had begun to contract because of the effects of the stock market and business crisis. A decline of 15 per cent between December, 1929, and December, 1930, would be comparison not with a high or a normal period, but with a level already influenced by the depression. The total decline would be the 15 per cent between December and December and the 5 per cent or so between December, 1929, and the preceding high. For the same reason a decline of 15 per cent between December and December might mean more unemployment than a decline of 20 per cent between November and November.

In other words, it is always necessary in a time series to determine whether comparisons with the preceding month or preceding year are with a normal, a high or a low level. Such comparisons are useful, but only if they are used with allowance for their possible error.

TABLE 5. INDEX NUMBERS OF FACTORY EMPLOYMENT, NEW YORK CITY
Average 1925–27 = 100
New York State Department of Labor

Month	1923	1924	1925	1926	1927	1928	1929	1930
January	115.2	109.3	101.7	102.4	98.6	90.9	89.0	87.7
February	116.1	110.8	104.9	103.6	100.2	91.6	91.3	87.7
March	119.0	111.4	107.0	104.6	101.0	93.1	93.8	89.2
April	117.4	107.8	103.7	102.7	98.7	90.7	92.7	87.0
May	115.4	103.2	101.6	99.1	96.0	88.6	90.5	84.2
June	113.2	101.1	100.9	98.6	95.1	87.4	89.7	81.9
July	111.9	98.8	99.3	95.1	92.6	86.3	88.4	78.2
August	110.8	98.1	99.8	96.4	94.2	87.6	90.2	79.6
September	112.3	103.7	102.9	100.2	97.0	90.6	94.0	83.3
October	115.6	104.6	104.6	102.3	97.4	92.7	95.6	82.8
November	113.6	103.5	103.6	101.3	95.7	91.4	93.1	79.9
December	110.1	103.1	103.3	100.3	93.6	90.6	89.4	77.0

A further complication in using reports for a given month is that each month normally represents a given level of seasonal activity quite apart from any cyclical changes.

Table 5 shows in detail the month to month changes in manufacturing employment in New York City. No average of these monthly figures was computed because it is not possible by that method to arrive at a normal seasonal curve. The changes in certain fundamental industrial procedures over the last ten years, and necessary administrative changes in the number of firms reporting to the New York State Department of Labor make such an average appear more satisfactory as arithmetic than it is as a picture of the economic process.

Briefly we may say that manufacturing in New York City is very low in January, with the closing down of the many lines dependent on Christmas business. It rises to a seasonal high in March, continuing into April if business is very good. May, June and July go progressively lower, and August shows the first signs of a normal upturn. October is the fall peak, with employment continuing high in November, if business is very good. December begins to be quite dull because most manufactured goods have moved into the dealers' hands for the retail business. A continuation of high activity beyond the usual busy months is a sign of good times, as much as a very high figure for the seasonal peak. A decline beginning early indicates bad business, as does a small seasonal increase in a normally busy period. The normal seasonal change from month to month in New York City, except perhaps for the September increase, stays within two per cent.

The other highly seasonal industries are those depending on the weather. Agriculture, of course, and building and road work, start in the early spring, rise to a peak through the late spring, summer, and early fall, and drop off considerably in the winter. A great many improvements in building technique have encouraged winter building, but they have not eliminated the seasonal movement.

The period of unemployment from the cold is greater for upstate New York than for New York City, so the workers who move upstate for agriculture and road work come into New York City fairly early in the fall.

This basic seasonal movement, as well as its effect upon the timing and duration of cyclical declines must be kept in mind in interpreting figures giving information about unemployment in New York City.

Employment in Factories, 1920–1930

Among the main industry groupings giving employment to the people of New York City—manufacturing, construction, trade, transportation, public service, personal service, the professions, and clerical work—it is possible to get definite information for the manufacturing industries alone.

The U. S. Census of Manufactures gives us the following information about the number of wage-earners in manufacturing in New York City. This classification, wage-earners, is smaller and less inclusive than the classification, gainfully employed, as used in the Census of Occupations.

The index of factory employment published in the monthly Industrial Bulletin of the New York State Department of Labor gives an index of 124 for the year 1919 and 130 for January of 1920, when the Census of Occupations was taken. This means that to get the num-

TABLE 6. WAGE-EARNERS IN MANUFACTURING, NEW YORK CITY
U. S. Census of Manufactures

Year	Number of establishments	Number of wage-earners
1914	29,621	585,279
1919	32,590	638,775
1921	26,801	536,665
1923	27,423[a][b]	577,971[a][b]
1925	23,714[a]	538,845[a]
1927	27,076[a]	552,507[a]

[a] The U. S. Census of Manufactures no longer includes very small firms with an annual product of less than $5,000. This change in procedure caused a reduction in the number of establishments covered after 1921 and a proportionately much smaller reduction in the number of employees reported on.

[b] From the U. S. Census of Manufactures, 1925; differs from number reported in Census for 1923 because of a revision. See U. S. Census of Manufactures, 1925, pp. 3–12.

ber employed in January, 1920, we have to add at least 5 per cent to allow for the rise in employment in the early part of the year. Furthermore, January is a month of seasonal unemployment so that more people would be attached to the manufacturing industries in January and reported as "gainfully employed" in the census than were actually on the payrolls of employers reporting to the State Department of Labor. In New York City manufacturing is greatly dependent on Christmas business and the multitude of small industries making leather belts, bags, novelties, paper boxes, etc., is very quiet in January. The fur garment shops and the candy factories also reduce their forces in good years and bad. If, then, we add 5 per cent to the Census of Manufactures figure of 638,775 wage-earners in 1919, we get 670,713 as wage-earners in January, 1920. We have to add also non-wage-earners attached to the industry—proprietors, managers, foremen, etc.—who are included in the Census of Occupations figure, estimated at an additional 10 per cent. We arrive, therefore, at an estimate of 740,000 "gainfully employed" in manufacturing in 1920.

Again taking the Census of Manufactures count of 552,507 wage-earners in 1927, and adding 10 per cent to allow for foremen, engineers, draftsmen, chemists, and other salaried workers who are not included in the figures for wage-earners and are included in the New York State index, we get an estimate for 1927 of 607,000. The Census of Occupations figures include employers and managers (who are relatively few) and exclude clerical and professional workers.

To get the estimate for 1929, we find a decline in the New York

State index from 96.7 for the year 1927 to 95.6 for October, the high point of 1929. This is a percentage decline of over one per cent. It gives us an estimate for the high of 1929 as 601,000. In October, 1930, the busy month of the fall season but otherwise under the full influence of the depression, we find a further drop in the index to 82.8, a decline of 12.8 points, or 13.4 per cent over October, 1929. In December, the dull season of 1930, the index had fallen to 77.0, a decline of 18.6 points, or 19.5 per cent, from October, 1929.

This means that by October, 1929, when employment was supposed to be at its peak for recent years, about 140,000 fewer people were employed in manufacturing than in 1920. That was before the depression began. Since that time another 80,000 were out even in the busiest part of 1930, and 119,000 were out in December, 1930.

TABLE 7. ESTIMATED NUMBER GAINFULLY EMPLOYED IN MANUFACTURING, NEW YORK CITY

Month and year	Gainfully employed	Decrease from previous date
January, 1920	740,000	
Average, 1927	607,000	133,000
October, 1929	601,000	6,000
October, 1930	520,466	80,534
December, 1930	483,805	36,661
Total		256,195

Two important considerations must be kept in mind in interpreting these figures. First, all such figures give the net displacement and not the total effect on the workers. All the various fluctuations in the separate industries are added together and their gains and losses cancelled in the figures, although obviously the hiring of 1,000 men in the printing of catalogues and calendars will not help the men or the women who are let go in the clothing industries. The number of workers released, therefore, is always very much larger than the net figures indicate, how much larger, no one knows. This is one source of the so-called "normal unemployment" which must be added to the volume of unemployment measured by employers' records alone.

The Normally Unemployed

Estimates of the number of people normally unemployed are again a matter of weighing imponderables. The gainfully employed in the United States exclusive of agriculture in 1920 were 30,661,090. Agriculture is excluded because so many of those gainfully employed are proprietors although some of the people included in the "normally unemployed" probably spend part of their time at least in agricultural work. Allowing for the same increase in the gainfully employed for the United States as a whole as took place in the general population, 16 per cent, we get an estimate for 1930 of 35,566,864, which is certainly not too high. "Normal unemployment" is one of the most controversial items in estimates of unemployment. Estimates made by Shelby Harrison and Hornell Hart give 5 per cent and 4.7 per cent as the lowest proportion of the unemployed population unemployed even in good years.[1]

Can we apply that same percentage to New York City to get its "normally unemployed"? The figure for the United States is probably too low for New York City for three reasons. New York City has a very large number of small industries and small plants, so that more variability in employment is covered in the net figures than is true of places with fewer lines of employment. Some of these industries dovetail. But the evidence of workers who are able to supplement earnings in one irregular industry by employment in another is very slight indeed.

Secondly, there has been plenty of evidence for years that the New York labor market was overcrowded. It is the port of debarkation for immigrants and the haven for thousands of people, young and old, from the North, the West, and the South. Because of the ease of getting workers quickly by inserting advertisements in the newspapers or through employment bureaus, employers inevitably tend to a less economical use of labor, so that many more workers have tended to congregate about the separate industries than could find full employment in them.[2] This is more like the situation in London than in the smaller cities of the United States, and is illustrated by the famous study of dock-workers by Mrs. Sidney Webb.[3]

Third, New York is also seasonally the refuge of men in irregular employment in the states around New York, who are attached to no locality. When they work, it is where roads are being built or reservoirs dug, or streams drained, sometimes in one county, some-

[1] Harrison, Shelby, *Public Employment Offices*, Russell Sage Foundation, New York, 1924, p. 8.
Hart, Hornell, *Fluctuations in Unemployment in Cities of the United States, 1902–1917*. Studies from Helen S. Trounstine Foundation, Cincinnati, Vol. I, No. 2, May 15, 1918.

[2] *Employment and Earnings of Men and Women in New York State Factories*, New York State Department of Labor, Special Bulletin No. 143, p. 20.

[3] Webb, Beatrice Potter (Mrs. Sidney Webb), *The Docks*, in Charles Booth's *Life and Labor in London*, First Series, Vol. IV, Chapter II, pp. 12–36.

times in another, but usually far from big cities. These men are not a responsibility of the town where they last worked but they are a responsibility of industry, of construction and road work, and engineering, and canning. They come to New York in the winter for the same reason that the money flows there—because it is an exchange, a market.

There is much protest because many of the men in breadlines have been working outside New York in the summer, and come here for the cold months. The protest is quite unjust. It is very bad for relief agencies and public officials to encourage migration and shift responsibility in hard times, but a failure to take the responsibility for men who are really employed in New York City industries, helping to create New York City's wealth, even though they may be working in the Adirondack Mountains, is equally bad.

If an estimate of four per cent were applied to New York's gainfully employed, we should have a "normal unemployment" in good years of 125,000. The minimum net unemployment in New York City, the irreducible minimum, is at least twice as high, or 250,000, and for the second reason mentioned above—the uneconomical use of labor in New York City industries. No one knows quite how high this may be. For most industries it has not been necessary to make a separate estimate of the normal unemployment for each industry, because we proceeded from census figures, not from payrolls. An estimate was made for manufacturing only because the data from the Census of Manufactures and the New York State Labor Department are based on employers' records and exclude the employment reserve of industry.

Declining Industries and Technological Unemployment

Even more important, this decline of at least 140,000 workers between 1920 and 1929, who certainly were not likely to find new jobs during the depression if they had not before, makes no allowance for the increase in population. The population of New York City increased over 20 per cent in nine years. If the workers in factories increased proportionately, we should have a population in factory industries not of 740,000 or 600,000, but 888,000. If all the new workers coming into industry from the schools, from immigration, and from the country, found their way into the expanding industries, they have not added to unemployment. But just so far as all manufacturing has drawn upon these new workers and let go its older or less skilled employees, it has increased by so much the number of people who were displaced in manufacturing, over and above the net decline in employment from 740,000 in 1920 to 600,000 at the busiest part of 1929.

Some of the 290,000 who would have been drawn into manufacturing if development there had been at the same pace as in the population as a whole undoubtedly found work in other industries like building maintenance, garage repair work, etc. Again, how many we cannot say. But we must remember that a considerable part of the "replacement" of workers in other jobs takes place within other manufacturing industries, and the figures above represent only the net displacement after eliminating all the additional men and women who found employment in the expanding manufacturing industries like the automobile, radio, electric apparatus, and building supply factories. These industries admittedly took up a large part of the slack left by industries reducing the demand for help, but the net reduction above remains after all the readjustments have been accounted for. Replacements in industry outside of manufacturing may have occurred in building, garage and service stations, radio installation, building maintenance, restaurants, and trade. But here also the people displaced in manufacturing, especially the older and less skilled workers, had to compete with the usual volume of new workers coming into industry, immigrants, people from the farms, and the increasing proportion of married women.

In this report increases and decreases for all industries except manufacturing are estimated as a whole, without separate estimates for the separate elements of demand. It is only in manufacturing where the official figures are based on employers' records and have to be adjusted for the number of workers dependent on these industries that the separate elements of unemployment must be estimated.

The best we can say, therefore, is that technological unemployment in the manufacturing industries probably did not go above 290,000 and certainly not much below 100,000 for manufacturing in New York City. It was probably much higher, assuming that the expanding manufacturing industries exerted their normal pull upon the new labor supply, and the manufacturing industries that were not expanding exerted some, but a smaller, pull in order to get the best labor available, and the lowest-priced labor for boys' and girls' jobs. And technological unemployment as such probably is less widespread in New York than in the rest of the country, because its greatest development has come in the large factories and the heavy industries, while here we tend to have small plants and light industries.

It is true that ever since the introduction of the factory system there have been problems of technological unemployment created by invention and by changes in demand. What seems to distinguish present conditions from those of the past is the systematic search for labor-saving machinery and the rapid and widespread installation both of mechanical devices and of scientific methods of organization. The problems of dislocation of employment seem to have increased in intensity during the last decade.

The estimates for manufacturing, then, are a minimum net unemployment due to cyclical conditions alone of 80,000 workers in the busy fall season of 1930 and of about 119,000 in December, with the prospect of a further drop of at least 10,000 in January, usually the low point of the manufacturing year. Over and above this we have the displacement of at least 100,000 workers in manufacturing alone, and above that the "normally unemployed," the minimum number who are out of work even in good times because our industries do not dovetail.

It is assumed that the effect of a falling demand for labor in good times is in part to distribute the smaller available amount of employment upon the entire group dependent on an industry or occupation. It leads, therefore, both to full unemployment for some, and greater irregularity of employment for others. To keep the estimates as conservative as possible, we have assumed that only half of those workers charged to changes in technology and long-time demand (above those who were replaced in other manufacturing industries) may be counted as unemployed. In strict justice this ought to lead to an increased estimate for the total number attached to the manufacturing industries to allow for the wide spread of partial employment, but again the more conservative figure has been taken.

Course of Employment in Manufacturing Compared with Other Industries

How far can we use the figures for manufacturing, which we have in considerable detail, as a basis for estimating unemployment in the other large occupational groups? Employment figures for non-manufacturing industries have been collected only within the last year or two, and are not available for New York State, but some idea of the movement of employment may be obtained by comparing the available figures for the Atlantic Division, and for Illinois and Wisconsin, although the dates are not exactly the same.

Employers' Reports from Other States

The reports from employers published by the U. S. Bureau of Labor Statistics for October, 1930, show a decline of 15 per cent from October, 1929, in employment in factories in the Atlantic Division.[1] The New York City figures for about the same period are 13 per cent. Of the other industries in the United States, wholesale trade shows a large decline, 8.5 per cent, retail trade and public utilities declined about 6 per cent, and hotels about 3 per cent. Steam railroads let out 14 per cent of their workers before the worst of the depression in August, and quarrying, which is somewhat of a guide to building activity, let out 18 per cent of its men.

TABLE 8. PER CENT CHANGE IN EMPLOYMENT AND PAYROLLS FROM OCTOBER, 1929, TO OCTOBER, 1930

U. S. Bureau of Labor Statistics[a]

Occupational group	Employment	Payrolls
Manufacturing, United States	−20.0	−28.9
Manufacturing, Middle Atlantic Division	−15.2	−23.3
Quarrying, United States	−18.2	−25.0
Public utilities, United States	−5.6	−4.5
Wholesale trade, United States	−8.5	−9.5
Retail trade, United States	−6.1	−7.3
Hotels, United States	−3.1	−4.7
Steam railroads, United States[b]	−14.0	−17.5

[a] *Monthly Labor Review*, U. S. Bureau of Labor Statistics, December, 1930, pp. 175–189.

[b] The comparisons are for August, 1929, and August, 1930. Since this study was completed corresponding figures for October have been published as follows: Employment −17.0, Payrolls −19.4.

In every industry group payroll declines were even greater, indicating that an additional 10 to 50 per cent of the workers were on part time. Also the decline in payrolls was steepest for the industries where the most men were let go. In public utilities there was less decline in payrolls than in employment, indicating either that wage scales were increased or, more likely, that the lower-paid men were let go.

Illinois and Wisconsin employment figures are given in the two accompanying tables. They give a clue to the decline in building employment between 1929 and 1930. They show 15 per cent and 13 per cent, respectively, from September, 1929, to September, 1930, a little less than the decline in manufacturing. This small decrease

[1] *Monthly Labor Review*, U. S. Bureau of Labor Statistics, December, 1930, p. 175.

may be due partly to the fact that a considerable decline in building work had already taken place before September, 1929. For New York City, however, we should expect a very much larger decline, because New York City was the mainstay of much of the building boom for the country as a whole. The expansion was so great that its deflation must be correspondingly greater. Building figures are the most difficult and unsatisfactory in the entire range of industries.

TABLE 9. INDEX NUMBERS OF EMPLOYMENT, ILLINOIS

Average 1925–27 = 100

Occupational group	Index numbers		Per cent change
	Sept., 1929	Sept., 1930	
Manufacturing	105.8	82.9	−21.6
Trade (wholesale and retail)	87.5	67.9	−22.4
Services			
Public utilities	107.4	100.2	−6.7
Building	84.9	72.4	−14.8

From *Monthly Labor Review*, U. S. Bureau of Labor Statistics, December, 1930, pp. 197–98.

For trade we get a percentage decline of 6 and 9 per cent for retail and wholesale trade in the United States from October to October. In Wisconsin we get 3 and 8 per cent and in Illinois, 22, from September to September. Illinois is a center for a big mail order business which depends upon the agricultural trade and which has been very greatly affected by both the low price of wheat and the drought. Otherwise Illinois would be much nearer New York City conditions than the reports for Wisconsin.

The U. S. Bureau of Labor Statistics gives no separate figure for transportation, but reports a decline of 6 per cent in employment in public utilities in the year ending in October, and of 14 per cent in steam railroads. Illinois shows a decline of 7 per cent in public utilities in the year ending in September. Wisconsin shows a decline of under 10 per cent for railroads, telephone and telegraph, and just over 10 per cent for light and power. Transportation in New York City includes the two very important elements of longshoremen and chauffeurs, so further evidence must be found for them.

The reports from other states cannot give us a basis for numerical estimates of the decline in employment in non-manufacturing industries in New York City, but they give us guide lines, above or below which the employment decline in New York City is likely to fall.

TABLE 10. INDEX NUMBERS OF EMPLOYMENT, WISCONSIN
Average 1925–27 = 100

Occupational group	Index numbers		Per cent change
	Sept., 1929	Sept., 1930	
Manual			
Manufacturing	101.3	83.1	−18.0
Construction			
Building	117.6	102.1	−13.2
Highway	138.4	137.5	−0.7
Railroad	133.1	92.4	−30.6
Marine and sewer	260.0	172.7	−33.6
Communication			
Steam railways	94.4	88.2	−6.6
Electric railways	67.9	61.2	−9.9
Express, telephone and telegraph	162.2	156.3	−3.6
Light and power	135.3	120.3	−11.1
Wholesale trade, manual	117.4	117.0	−0.3
Hotels and restaurants	101.8	85.2	−16.3
Laundrymen	117.1	106.7	−8.9
Non-manual			
Construction	99.5	99.0	−0.5
Communication	117.9	117.0	−0.8
Wholesale trade	112.9	104.0	−7.9
Retail, sales force	115.3	112.2	−2.7
Miscellaneous professional	127.6	115.5	−9.5

From *Monthly Labor Review*, U. S. Bureau of Labor Statistics, December, 1930, p. 200.

Unemployment Census of Buffalo

A further and quite distinct type of collateral evidence about unemployment in the separate industries of New York City is furnished by the house to house survey of wage-earners in Buffalo made by Frederick E. and Fred C. Croxton[1] and the New York State Department of Labor. It is important to remember that all studies based on manufacturers' payroll records include only those who are engaged in any industry in any given period. It does not include the industrial periphery, the workers who are dependent on a given industry for work but who may not be on any particular employer's payroll at a given time, and who cannot all be employed at any one time, because they constitute the reserve of industry from which are recruited the extra people for busy seasons, expanding industries or operations, and all the other adjustments that industries are constantly making. This reserve is counted in any census of the unemployed and, therefore, the difference between

[1] *Unemployment in Buffalo, November, 1930*, New York State Department of Labor, Special Bulletin No. 167.

total labor supply and numbers actually at work in a period of depression is greater than between the maximum number employed at one time in good years and the number at work in bad times, as reported from employers' payrolls. The Buffalo figures represent actual counts of about 5 per cent of the gainfully employed persons in Buffalo, in carefully selected representative districts. The figures for the separate industries are given in Tables 11 and 12.

TABLE 11. PER CENT OF FULL-TIME, PART-TIME, AND NO EMPLOYMENT, BUFFALO, 1929 AND 1930—MEN ONLY

Industry group	1929			1930		
	Employed full time	Employed part time	Unemployed all causes	Employed full time	Employed part time	Unemployed, able and willing to work[a]
Professional service............	90.9	4.5	4.6	91.2	2.3	4.6
Domestic and personal service.	86.5	3.2	10.3	73.5	8.4	15.8
Government employees (other than teachers)............	89.5	2.6	7.9	79.1	5.8	7.7
Trade and transportation.....	90.2	2.9	6.9	73.0	11.0	12.3
Retail and wholesale trade..	90.4	2.3	7.3	75.8	8.1	13.5
Telephone and telegraph....	94.9	..	5.1	86.4	2.9	9.7
Railway express, gas, electric light...............	90.5	2.7	6.8	69.1	14.9	10.8
Water transportation......	74.4	12.2	13.4	54.6	16.1	29.3
Other....................	90.4	4.1	5.5	80.2	5.9	11.3
Manufacturing and mechanical pursuits.................	77.3	10.3	12.4	47.9	27.1	21.4
Building trades, contractors	63.7	16.3	20.0	39.5	19.7	30.1
Building trades, wage-earners....................	68.0	9.3	22.7	44.9	17.1	33.5
Self-employed..............	88.0	3.5	8.5	82.6	5.8	5.5
Miscellaneous..............	72.2	1.9	25.9	23.9	4.4	54.3
All occupations[b]............	82.4	6.7	10.9	61.4	17.8	16.5

From *Unemployment in Buffalo, November, 1930*, New York State Department of Labor, Special Bulletin No. 167, p. 39.

[a] The remainder, about 3.6 per cent, includes those unable to work, or those not seeking work, such as building contractors, retired government workers, etc.

[b] Total includes more items than those given above.

How far, however, may Buffalo conditions be taken as similar to conditions in New York City? Buffalo is a city of heavy manufacturing industries, of transportation and considerable trade. New York City has more light manufacturing, and much more transportation, more clerical work, more building, and more trade in proportion to its population. Buffalo has had a large influx of population from the country districts to heavy manufactures and chemical industries. On the other hand, it has probably not nearly so large a labor pool as New York City—not so many people attached to each industry, who can never all be employed at one time. New York City has more seasonal displacement, and the uneconomical use of labor referred to above.

TABLE 12. PER CENT OF FULL-TIME, PART-TIME, AND SLACK WORK, BUFFALO, 1930—MEN AND WOMEN

Industry group	Employed full time	Employed part time	Unemployed, able and willing to work[a]
Professional service	89.5	3.4	5.1
Domestic and personal service	65.0	13.6	19.2
Government employees (other than teachers)	79.6	5.8	7.6
Trade and transportation	75.2	10.0	11.8
Retail and wholesale	77.1	8.4	12.6
Telephone and telegraph	86.0	4.8	8.8
Railway, express, gas and electric light	69.9	14.3	10.7
Water transportation	54.0	16.0	30.0
Other	82.6	4.7	10.5
Manufacturing and mechanical pursuits	49.1	26.4	21.2
Building trades, contractors	39.5	19.7	30.1
Building trades, wage-earners	45.6	16.9	33.1
Labor (not otherwise specified)	16.7	26.2	35.7
Self-employed	83.7	6.0	4.9
Miscellaneous	24.2	3.1	59.4
All occupations[b]	63.7	16.7	16.0

From *Unemployment in Buffalo, November, 1930*, New York State Department of Labor, Special Bulletin, No. 167, p. 39.

[a] The remainder, about 3.6 per cent, includes those unable to work, or those not seeking work, such as building contractors, retired government workers, etc.

[b] Total includes more items than those given above.

Construction

Employment in Construction, 1929

Before arriving at the number of people out of work in each industrial group other than manufacturing in New York City, we shall have to estimate the total number of people available for employment in 1929.

For construction work it is easier to arrive at a direct estimate of the labor supply at present than to derive an estimate from the census figures of 1920, which combine manufacturing and construction. To get the 1929 figure from the Census of Occupations in 1920, we should have to start from the money value of plans filed or contracts let for building construction for 1920 and for the recent peak.

The valuation of plans[1] filed for 1929 was more than three times as great as for 1920 and the valuation of actual contracts let rose even more. This is indirectly related to the demand for building labor, but the indirections include changes in the value of money, changes in the cost of building materials and of building labor—and, therefore, the ratio of labor cost to total cost—and also in the varying margin of unused labor, the use of overtime, winter employment, the substitution of machinery and possible resistance by the trade unions to permitting the labor supply to expand at the rate desired by employers. The supply of building labor certainly did not expand in anything like the ratio of building work measured in money. It expanded as little as the economizing of labor by employers and the resistance to expansion by unions made possible. It is unwise to attempt an estimate with so many factors of unknown weight.

But there are available estimates of the supply of building workers at present (December, 1930) in New York City. These are better than a complicated series of estimates derived from 1920 figures. An official of the Building Trades Federation estimated 154,000 organized building workers, and the Building Congress estimated an additional 50,000 unorganized workers. This is the best available estimate of the supply of people looking for jobs in construction.

Unemployment in Construction, 1930

The New York State Labor Department in the Industrial Bulletin for December, 1930, gives the total valuation of projected building work in New York City as follows:

Period	Estimated valuation, all building projects including alterations
11 months, 1928	$877,415,000
11 months, 1929	919,840,000
11 months, 1930	382,023,000

From *Industrial Bulletin*, New York State Department of Labor, December, 1930, p. 99. Based on plans filed with the Building Departments of the five boroughs and compiled by the New York State Department of Labor.

Building projects went down almost 60 per cent in money value between 1929 and 1930. These changes have some index value for labor conditions. It is easier to assume a correspondence between em-

[1] Compiled by the New York State Department of Labor from reports received from the building departments of the five boroughs. Figures for 1920 were published in the *Labor Market Bulletin*, New York State Department of Labor, 1920, and figures for 1929 were published in the *Industrial Bulletin*, New York State Department of Labor, 1929.

ployment and building plans within a two-year period than over ten years as filled with new experiments and shifts in industry as was the decade from 1920 to 1930. The decline is chiefly in residential construction, most of which would be built by organized labor. Since some building projects last a year or more, there is considerable lag in the effect of the volume of plans on building employment, and the employment decline, therefore, must have been somewhat under 60 per cent.

The figures for building contracts actually awarded, compiled by the F. W. Dodge Corporation, publishers of the General Building Contractor, are assumed to be closer to the immediate demand for employment in construction than are the figures for new projects filed with the building department.[1] According to the F. W. Dodge figures, contracts let in December, 1930, were 60 per cent lower than the average of the five preceding Decembers. Contracts let for the whole year 1930 were 29 per cent less than contracts let in the year 1929. The year's figures are a better indication of employment levels than the figures for any one month because building projects mean employment over many months, but the trend is sometimes better indicated by the recent figures. New building is apparently not coming along to take the place of those projects which were begun even in the early months of 1930.

The unemployment study for Buffalo, in which unemployment is computed on the available labor supply, not on the maximum number employed, indicates that one-third of the building workers in Buffalo had no employment in 1930 and another sixth worked only part-time. That is equivalent to a total unemployment approaching 40 per cent.

In making our estimate of the number unemployed in the construction industries in New York City we have the following estimates to guide us—total unemployment of 30 per cent of the workers (excluding part-time) in Buffalo in December, 1930; a decline of 15 per cent in numbers employed in Illinois in September; a decline of 13 per cent in building employment, practically no change in highway construction, and 30 per cent in railroad and sewer building in Wisconsin; a decline of 39 per cent for the country as a whole in the estimate of the Standard Statistics Company,[2] a decline of almost 60 per cent in the value of plans filed in the eleven months of 1930, which—allowing for the lag between building plans and build-

---

[1] For current summaries of the F. W. Dodge figures, see the *Monthly Review of Credit and Business Conditions*, New York Federal Reserve Bank.

[2] See Table 15, p. 51.

ing employment—means a decline of at least 30 per cent in employment; and also a decline of about 30 per cent in contracts let in 1930 compared with 1929. We have also the fact that the building boom and, therefore, the pressure for the expansion of labor in New York City was much greater than for the country as a whole. All these facts together justify us in taking the special census figures of Buffalo, which show a decline in employment of 33.1 as a conservative estimate for New York City building workers, exclusive of contractors.[1]

It is not always possible to separate entirely workers in special construction—roughly identical with the unorganized workers—and building contractors. The largest project in non-building construction is the new subway. In December, 1929, the contractors working on the subway employed, according to the reports of the Transit Commission, 11,513 men.[2] In December, 1930, the number had dropped to 9,475, a decline of 18 per cent.[3] The next question is whether that 18 per cent is typical of non-building construction or too high or too low. Under ordinary circumstances, large expenditures for new plant and engineering projects are likely to be suspended abruptly in a depression. This year President Hoover has particularly urged that employers and large corporations try to plan their new construction to take up some of the slack of the depression. Giving full allowance to that possibility, we can, therefore, take 15 per cent as indicating the decline in that type of work. That is about half the decline in building construction, and appears, therefore, very conservative. The reports on contracts let for public works and utilities in New York City compiled by the F. W. Dodge Corporation indicate a reduction of about 40 per cent in estimated cost of building projects for the entire year 1930 compared with 1929.

These estimates of unemployment are based on the demand for building workers as measured by contracts for 1929. In building, however, the recent peak demand came in 1928. Although plans remained high, the valuation of contracts actually let went definitely lower. A very large number of workers were already unable in 1929 to find employment in the industry in which they were employed

[1] After the study was completed, an official of the Building Trades Employers' Association estimated that 40 per cent of the organized building workers in New York City were unemployed on February 2. This also is a conservative estimate and indicates that the percentage of 33⅓ unemployed in December is certainly not too high in view of the fact that the weather so far has been mild enough to have furnished no seasonal interference with building.

[2] *Transit Record*, Board of Transportation of New York City, January, 1930.

[3] *Ibid.*, January, 1931.

the preceding year. Labor is used to these constant shifts in employment and makes an adjustment which is adequate enough so that their distress is not forced on public attention. Here again, however, is the source of that "normal unemployment" which keeps a much larger number of people attached to an industry than can ever attain full employment in it. Workers do not have access to building contract figures. Their natural tendency, when one job is finished, is to seek employment in another building project. It is not the natural inclination of employers to encourage them to find a more active industry. As the demand for labor goes down, employment tends to be distributed unevenly among the people clustered about an industry. It is probable, therefore, that there was an additional number of people, employed in building work in 1928, who had not readjusted themselves in another industry by 1929. This would apply particularly to the non-union workers employed chiefly on large engineering projects.

Building Contractors

Building contractors are to be counted among the unemployed, as well as wage-earners, when the classification fits. A very large proportion of building contractors are men employing one or two men, and often working at their trade themselves. That is one reason why it is so hard to get adequate figures for building work. The Buffalo study indicates that about 28 per cent of the building workers were independent contractors. That percentage is too high for New York City, where large projects mean more capitalization and larger organizations. Assuming the number of building contractors is not more than one-fifth as large as the number of organized workers, we get about 30,000 men. In the Buffalo study, unemployment was as common among them as among the regular craftsmen. Probably they are not all so dependent on immediate earnings as to be called unemployed when work ceases. Profits from good times are the fund from which the enterpriser carries himself through hard times. It is only when the independent contractor works on so small a scale that his payment is practically wages, when it is hardly a capitalistic enterprise at all, that his lack of business becomes unemployment. The Buffalo estimate of 30 per cent unemployed among contractors is then reduced to 10 per cent even though the Buffalo study counted separately those building contractors "not looking for work," and reported a very high figure (7 per cent) among building contractors compared with other self-employed occupational groups.

Other Industries

The remaining groups of occupations for which we must estimate the labor supply in 1929 and the unemployment in 1930 are transportation, trade, public service, professional service, domestic and personal service, and clerical work. There is no definite set of figures for any of these groups. The best we can do is to find the material on such subdivisions of each group as may have been reported upon, to establish a prevailing percentage change for the remainder of each group, and to make such allowance in establishing this percentage change as is made necessary by the degree to which special conditions differ in New York City from those for the nation as a whole.

Rate of Normal Growth, 1920–29

The net increase in population for New York City between 1920 and 1930 was 23 per cent. This is slightly above 2 per cent a year. In the absence of other evidence, therefore, we shall take the normal rate of growth from 1920 through 1929 as 20 per cent, about 2 per cent a year. This corresponds conservatively with the familiar estimates of about 3 per cent a year as the normal rate of growth in industry and in currency requirements.

Transportation

In the census group for transportation, New York City is distinguished by the large proportion of longshoremen, sailors, chauffeurs, teamsters, garage workers, telephone and telegraph operators, and employees in street railroad transportation. (See Table 13).

We can get some idea of the drop in employment for longshore workers in the last year from the Buffalo figures. They show unemployment of 30 per cent in water transportation in Buffalo. On the other hand, one of the longshoremen's local unions in New York City reported that 75 per cent of its members were idle. Longshore work is subject in the best of times to a high rate of unemployment.[1] The Port of New York has a very large volume of foreign commerce, whereas the bulk of the work at Buffalo is local transportation. We know that foreign commerce has been very greatly reduced during the past year because of the world-wide character of the depression and the upsetting effect of the change in the tariff law. The New

---

[1] *Report of Dock Employment in New York City and Recommendations for its Regularization*, Mayor's Committee on Unemployment, New York City, October, 1916, p. 17.
Barnes, Charles B., *The Longshoreman*, Survey Associates, 1915, Chapt. V, pp. 55–75.

York Federal Reserve Bank in its Monthly Review reports a fall of 25 per cent in exports for November, 1930, from November, 1929, and almost as much in imports.[1] These are in dollar values and the volume of goods handled would not have decreased so much, but, on the other hand, November of 1929 had already begun to show the downward tendency. It is likely that the unemployment rate for longshoremen in New York City is higher than the 30 per cent for water transportation in Buffalo but probably closer to the Buffalo figure than to that reported by the one trade union. We may, therefore, take 50 per cent as the proportion of unemployed longshoremen in New York City. In the absence of more definite figures, there is reason to suppose that the rate of growth of the labor supply in the longshore industry between 1920 and 1929 was slightly less than the average rate of growth of the wage-earning population of 20 per cent. Where the number of laborers was so far in excess of those needed, it was possible to expand operations considerably without drawing in new workers.

Among sailors, about the same conditions would prevail, except that the normal reserve of workers, that proportion who can never all obtain work at any one time, is much less for sailors than for the longshore industry. We can, therefore, reduce the unemployment percentage to 25. We must also reduce the rate of growth for the decade because 1920 was a year of great activity on the part of American shipping, left over from war activities. The depression of 1921 hit the shipping industries of the United States quite severely, and in the recovery that followed probably more workers were drawn into the land industries that were expanding rapidly than into shipping. The estimate of 25 per cent unemployment for sailors corresponds also with the 29 per cent unemployment for water transportation used in the estimate of the Standard Statistics Company, published October 15, 1930. Probably New York City is also the market where unemployed sailors attached to other ports are likely to congregate to learn of the few available jobs.

For teamsters and chauffeurs, we have two estimates of local unions. One reported 60 per cent of its members out of work and the other reported 40 per cent. In Buffalo, trade and transportation altogether were reported as showing a decline of 11.8 per cent. Since this includes some very stable elements of trade and transportation, like the telephone and telegraph and electric light industries, the decline in a volatile group like chauffeurs and teamsters must cer-

[1] *Monthly Review of Credit and Business Conditions*, New York Federal Reserve Bank, January, 1931, p. 7.

tainly be much greater than 12 per cent. It seems as if unemployment of 20 per cent for this group would be an extremely conservative estimate. In arriving at the labor supply for these two occupations in 1929, we have to allow for an increase of much more than 20 per cent since 1920 for chauffeurs and something less than 20 per cent for draymen and teamsters, although there has been a turn in the movement to replace horse transportation by mechanical transportation for certain types of delivery work, especially where there is a good deal of waiting time. We can, therefore, assume an increase among chauffeurs of at least 25 per cent between 1920 and 1929 and an increase for teamsters of about 10 per cent.

Garage and road laborers are an occupational group which increased in numbers very greatly over the 1920 level. We can assume a 40 per cent rate of growth for them on the theory that in New York City they are mostly garage workers. Automobile manufacture has expanded more than most industries in the United States. Automobile servicing, of course, grows in relation to the accumulated number of cars and not merely in relation to the growth in production in any one year.

With a general unemployment rate in Buffalo of 16 per cent, we must assume unemployment among garage laborers to be above the line indicating the average. We can, therefore, assume a recent decline of at least 20 per cent, the same figure as for chauffeurs and teamsters. This census classification excludes the two types of people in garage servicing whose employment would be most stable —the proprietors and the skilled mechanics.

Telephone and telegraph operators include employees in the public service companies, in general business, and, in New York City, an important group in stock exchange and brokerage work. Employment in the large public service companies has apparently not decreased, although it has also probably failed to show the normal rate of growth between 1929 and 1930. The introduction of the dial telephone system in New York City has meant that placement workers in employment offices have been left with a large group of people coming into the labor market whom they formerly placed with the Telephone Company but for whom they could not now get such positions, apart from the effects of the depression. We can assume, therefore, no increase in the number of telephone workers in the public service companies, a decline smaller than the general average in ordinary business and a large decline in stock exchange and brokerage work. This gives us about 7 per cent as the unemployment for telephone and 10 per cent for telegraph operators.

In order to get at an estimate of the workers attached to the telephone and telegraph industries in 1929, we must allow for a greater increase in telephone usage than in population, a growing economy in the use of employees in telephone work, and a considerable economizing of labor in telegraphy because of the introduction of labor-saving devices. If, however, we include the gain in workers employed in radio occupations, we can assume that the combined group of telegraph and radio workers (apart from salesmen, etc.), has increased at least 15 per cent. For telephone operators, we can assume 30 per cent as including the increase above the growth in population, even with the maximum economy in the use of operators.

For street railroad transportation we have exact figures from the New York Transit Commission. Full-time workers decreased slightly for the nine years, and part-time workers increased. Street railroad and subway operation has been subject to extreme economizing in the use of labor, partly because of the effects of the agitation over the five-cent fare, and by means of one-man cars, automatic door-closing machinery, and similar devices. Employment had increased slightly for full-time workers in June, 1930, over June, 1929. June, however, was part of the brief recovery of business early in 1930. Part-time work had gone down markedly. It is likely that the shrinkage in the movement of population that would have followed the decreased employment in the second half of 1930 would have made it unnecessary for the companies to hire many men, even to make replacements for the ordinary losses in working forces. That is, it is the natural inference that the decline in employment in street railway work by December would have been greater than that recorded by June. The companies endeavor to distribute work among the men attached to the industry, giving them all some employment and smaller earnings. The visiting nurse associations are finding more calls from street railway employees because of their reduced earnings. But even with a policy of distributing available work, the number of men employed will continue to decline because the companies do not make full replacements, and of course, they do not undertake the normal annual expansion.

For the remaining group of transportation, all others, we can take the "normal" percentage increase, 20 per cent, to get the approximate 1929 labor supply. To get at the decline for 1930, we have as guides the Wisconsin figures, which show a decrease of from 4 per cent to 10 per cent for "communication" in September, and the Buffalo figures, which give about 12 per cent for transportation in November. The Buffalo figures include the very high percentage for water transportation, but the number in the group is very small. We arrive, therefore, at about ten per cent, a little less than the Buffalo percentage, of unemployment.

Trade

To get at an estimate of the increase in the number of occupied persons engaged in trade between 1920 and 1929, we have no direct information. The census of distribution will give us data when that is completed. We have, of course, the 20 per cent which measures the growth in total population and can assume that trade grows faster than population in a highly commercialized city in the center of a large purchasing area like New York City. Trade grows in New York City because the growth of communication increases the number of people who can reach a central market, the increase in general wealth causes more people to want to reach the luxury market, and the increase in gainful employment, urbanization in general, causes people to get more of their goods and services through purchases from the market rather than through the efforts of themselves or their families. For these reasons, we are assuming that in most branches of trade growth was much more rapid than growth in population as a whole. It is, of course, true that the expansion in trade, measured in sales figures, is greater than the expansion in the number of people engaged in trade.

Wholesale dealers we know were becoming somewhat less important in the scheme of distribution for commodities affected by the chain-store method. They are, therefore, given a percentage increase smaller than that of other people engaged in trade.

To get at the volume of unemployment in 1930, we can assume that "wholesale dealers," including managers, were virtually all "employed." This again is taking the most conservative possible estimate.

Among retail dealers, there is a considerable proportion engaged in very small businesses and virtually earning wages. Some part of these people have probably been thrown on the labor market.

For employment in trade in general, we have a decline of 22 per cent reported in Illinois in September, influenced in part by the effect of the agricultural depression in mail order houses. We have also a decline of 8 per cent or less for wholesale trade in Wisconsin in September and the total unemployment of 12.6 per cent for Buffalo in November. For trade and service combined, the Standard Statistics Company found a decline of 11 per cent for the United

States in September. The Buffalo figures bear out the *a priori* assumption that trade is the more stable, and service the more variable, element of the combination.

So far as we can estimate the degree to which New York City figures would differ from those for other sections of the country, it is probable that wholesale trade in New York City would show wider fluctuations in employment, because it is the farthest removed from retailing. It includes more of the trade that is closest to the producer and, therefore, midway between the wide fluctuations of raw materials and the comparative stability of retail trade. In retail trade also, we have to allow for greater variability in New York City, partly because a smaller proportion of trade here tends to be in groceries and other staples, and more in clothing and specialties. Also, New York has a very, very high proportion of the luxury elements in all the branches of trade. In clothing, in jewelry, in decorations, etc., it has the most expensive and select shops, where increases and declines are more extreme than in medium and low-priced goods. On both counts, therefore, because of the proportion of business in clothing and specialties as against necessities, and because of the proportion catering to luxurious standards of expenditure, New York would experience more irregularity than the country as a whole.

Very carefully compiled figures for trade in the metropolitan area indicate that department store sales in New York City in 1930 compared well in money value with sales in 1929.[1] Allowing for such decline in price as has taken place, the volume of department store sales in the reporting firms in the New York district in 1930 must, therefore, have been above that for 1929. It would appear, however, that this phenomenon must indicate the transfer of a very large amount of purchasing from specialty shops to department stores during the depression, either as a result of their price policy or for some other reason.

Retail trade in the fields included in department store activities has been very severely affected by the depression. Specialty shops and those appealing to people of considerable wealth have been most affected. Apparently, as in the case of restaurants, transactions tend to move down the line so that many people who formerly went to the highest-priced shops go to the next lower level, and each level of shops, except those at the top, receives people from above and loses some to the level below. In this readjustment, only those

---

[1] *Monthly Review of Credit and Business Conditions*, New York Federal Reserve Bank, January, 1931, p. 8.

stores benefit which, like the five and ten cent stores, or department stores emphasizing the appeal to price in their advertising, draw in a large new clientele which is in a mood for the appeal to price. That is to say, the gain in department store sales, while an interesting phenomenon, cannot be used to prove either that the volume of retail trade in clothing, furniture, etc., is as high as that of 1929, or that expenditures for sales help have been as high as in 1929.

Furthermore, we must assume here also that figures for the total volume of unemployment will be considerably larger than figures showing a change in total sales in 1930 over 1929. The stock market depression came in October and, in the following months of 1929, reduced purchasing had already seriously affected stores catering to luxury purchasers. For these reasons we are starting from the Buffalo census figure for November and the Standard Statistics Company estimate, which show a volume of 12 per cent unemployment for wholesale and retail trade, and assuming that the rise in sales help in New York in December over November about compensates for the greater variability of trade in New York City compared with that in the country as a whole. We are taking, therefore, 12 per cent as the decline in the "all others" group and at least 9 per cent as the figure for clerks in stores. Here also we must assume that a very large reduction in employment will have taken place between December and January.

Wholesale trade in the New York City district had declined about 24 per cent in November, 1930, compared with November, 1929.[1] Wholesale trade always shows a greater amplitude of variation than retail trade but a 24 per cent decline in wholesale trade seems to indicate considerable decline in retail trade.

The New York Federal Reserve Bank reports an average decline of 15 per cent in 1930 from 1929, for ten series of items covering various fields of trade. Car loadings, which are often taken as an index of trade activity, declined 12 per cent.[2] Here again we must allow for two facts, that changes in the volume of trade mean a smaller change either up or down in volume of employment dependent upon trade, and secondly, that percentage comparisons showing the decline from last year fail to take into consideration either so much decline in employment as had already taken place at the end of last year or such reserve of unemployment as is true of all industries, sometimes even at the peak of their activity.

[1] *Monthly Review of Credit and Business Conditions*, New York Federal Reserve Bank, January, 1931, p. 8.
[2] *Ibid.*, p. 5.

In banking, insurance, and real estate, there was undoubtedly some shrinkage in employment, both from the diminishing volume of business in the stock market and in trade, and from the strong tendency on the part of hard-pressed employers to economize in the use of workers from the top to the bottom of an organization as a result of decreased income during the period of depression. We have assumed a nominal decline of 5 per cent since a large proportion of the people in these occupations belong to the most permanent part of the working staff.

Delivery men in stores, we have assumed, were affected by about the same conditions as chauffeurs and teamsters generally, except that they represent the more stable half of a very irregularly employed occupation.

Public Service

Under public service, the Census of Occupations includes only occupations like watchmen, policemen, etc., which are peculiarly public in their nature. We have, however, exact figures of the number of employees in the New York City Government for 1920[1] and 1929.[2] These figures include clerks and professional workers, classified elsewhere by the Census of Occupations, but do not include school teachers. All the employees reported by the New York City Government are included under public service for convenience of reference. The remainder of the group in public service, therefore, includes guards, watchmen, soldiers and sailors, and federal and state employees, except clerks. They may be assumed to have had a rate of growth a little higher than that for the total population. They are reported in the table without change between 1929 and 1930.

The employment figures for the city employees for 1930 are not yet available. It was the estimate of the Chief Examiner of the New York City Civil Service Commission that the figures would show a very slight increase. There is in every year, except where there is some very unusual circumstance, an increase in the number of workers in the civil service. There is, of course, no corresponding elimination of workers in hard times. Because of the additional work entailed by the establishment of old-age pensions in New York City, as well as the normal rate of growth, allowance is made for an increase between 1929 and 1930 of 2 per cent.

Professional Service

In professional service in New York City, actors, musicians and teachers provide the principal groups which can be separated out.

[1] New York City, Civil Service Commission, Annual Report, 1920, p. 12.
[2] *Ibid.*, 1929, p. 14.

All three grew at a rate very much faster than the increase in the normal population. The amusement industry was one of the conspicuous examples of expansion in the last decade, and school attendance has also increased greatly.

We can, therefore, make an estimate of at least 30 per cent increase for the separate groups under professional service. For unemployment in 1930, however, we have to allow for the fact that musicians have just been conspicuously exposed to the results of the substitution of machinery for human skill, that is, technological unemployment. It has not been possible to get an exact estimate of the number of musicians unemployed. It was enough, however, before the depression began to have reached very serious consequences, especially among the employees in the orchestras of moving picture theaters. Teachers of music have also been very seriously affected by the depression, but it has probably been mostly in the form of a reduced volume of work rather than direct unemployment.

Teachers in the public schools and in private schools have probably suffered very little displacement. Teachers in universities and in adult education generally have felt the effect of the smaller amount of money which people have had to spend on luxuries like education.

The Buffalo study showed an unemployment ratio of 5 per cent for professional workers. Wisconsin has a group, "miscellaneous professional workers," in which unemployment in September was already 10 per cent. In most professional occupations, it is likely that unemployment is not much more than 5 per cent. The Mayor's Committee on Unemployment, in its 1916 Report, spoke of a large volume of unemployment in professional work.[1] Allowance must be made here, however, for the fact that so many professional and semi-professional workers are self-employed. They usually meet with a reduction in working time and in income rather than with total unemployment.

Actors in the theater have felt the effect of diminished purchasing power. Actors in moving pictures may have felt the effect of a lessened production of new pictures or they may not. Among the trade unions that could give an estimate of the number of members unemployed, only one reported no unemployment. That was the moving picture operators union. The union of laboratory workers in the moving picture industry reported unemployment of 4 per cent, which is about the normal reserve of most industries even in good times.

[1] *Report of Mayor's Committee on Unemployment*, New York City, January, 1916, p. 12.

Domestic and Personal Service

Four industries in which there was a more than normal increase in business between 1920 and 1929 are included in the group "domestic and personal service." They are hairdressers, elevator operators, laundry operatives, and waiters. All four occupations grew in response to increased purchasing power, and the growing demand for personal service as people worked away from home, as more married women worked, and as people worked longer distances from home and had less time to do things for themselves. The estimate of the Standard Statistics Company on employment for 1929 gave 12,522,000 workers in the United States in trade and service combined.[1] The U. S. Census of Occupations for 1920 gave 7,648,000 workers in the two groups. If these figures cover the same employees, as they appear to do, this gives an estimate of well over 50 per cent as the increase in trade and service for the United States as a whole between 1920 and 1929. The increase was unquestionably greater in New York City, where there is so strong a tendency toward large units in building, both for business and private use, which require more specialized personal service. Here again, however, a conservative estimate was used in Table 13.

In the decline in employment, waiters probably suffered most severely, with cleaning women and hairdressers next. The Buffalo figure for "domestic and personal service" showed unemployment of 19.2 per cent in November. The New York group of similar workers ought to be more variable because they include a larger margin of luxury expenses and items of expenditure that have grown up as a matter of convenience, when money was plentiful, and can be contracted when money is not so easily obtained—that is, meals away from home, special services, etc.

The U. S. Bureau of Labor Statistics found a decline of 3 per cent in hotels for the United States from October, 1929, to October, 1930. That is obviously too low for New York City, where the multiplicity of hotel services leaves much more room for contraction of employment. In Wisconsin, hotels and restaurants together showed a decline of 16 per cent by September, 1930. The Standard Statistics Company estimated a drop of 11 per cent for trade and service combined in September in the United States, and in that average, domestic and personal service was likely to show more variation than trade, that is, to come above rather than below the average. Barbers and hairdressers are assumed to include many proprietors,

---

[1] See Table 15, p. 51.

so that the rate for the group as a whole would be much lower than the rate for employed hairdressers and barbers.

Clerical Occupations

For the clerical workers in New York City we have definite information about a considerable group employed by the gas and electrical industries and subject to the Public Service Commission. We must also make an adjustment for a large number of clerical workers who are employed by New York City and included in the New York City official figures but not classified as clerical workers by the Census of Occupations.

For the remaining workers in clerical occupations, we have to estimate the increase in employment through 1929 and the decline since that date. It is reasonable to assume that clerical occupations increased in New York City faster than the population as a whole because that is the effect of increasing commercialization, of which New York City is the extreme example. Furthermore, the extension of grammar school and high school education to more and more people has had the effect of sending them into clerical occupations much faster than the demand for their services rose. The supply of people available for clerical work has probably increased at least twice as fast as the general population.

In estimating the unemployment in 1930 in clerical work, a large amount of technological unemployment, very much greater than most people have yet recognized, must be borne in mind. Clerical work, like manufacturing, has been subject to the increasing use of labor-saving machinery and also the tendency of employers greatly to economize on labor because of the incidental expenses that are saved in addition to the direct wage-saving involved.[1]

It is probable that clerical work had expanded greatly in the period before 1920 and that the economies introduced by the depression of 1921 and the movement for a careful study of personnel left much room for contraction in the number of people who could obtain jobs without in the least decreasing the supply. The unemployment ratio of 15 per cent for the clerical industries is the general figure for the contraction in the volume of all transactions. It is very true that clerical work on the whole is likely to be much more

[1] Even in 1915 the Mayor's Committee on Unemployment said, "An unusually high rate for clerical and professional pursuits is evident." This was before the two special circumstances mentioned here were fully operative, that is, the spread of technological economizing of labor to clerical work and the oversupply of clerical workers by the school system. *Report of Mayor's Committee on Unemployment*, New York City, January, 1916, p. 12.

TABLE 13. ESTIMATED NUMBER UNEMPLOYED IN NEW YORK CITY, DECEMBER, 1930, BY OCCUPATIONAL GROUPS

Occupational group	Gainfully employed			Estimated unemployment, December, 1930	
	Number, 1920 Census of Occupations	Estimated per cent change, 1920 to 1929	Estimated number, 1929	Per cent	Number
Construction	..	..	234,000	..	62,093
Organized	..	..	154,000	33.3	51,282
Subway construction	..	..	11,513[a]	17.7[c]	2,038[a]
Other, unorganized	..	..	38,487	15.0	5,773
Contractors, etc.	..	..	30,000	10.0	3,000
Manufacturing	794,182[b]	..	776,447	..	212,195
Employers' reports	740,000[b]	−18.8[c]	601,000	19.5[c]	117,195
Normal unemployment	37,000[d]	+21.6[c]	45,000[d]	100.0	45,000
Increase reserve due to technological unemployment	..	..	100,000	50.0	50,000
Gas and electricity	17,182[e]	+77.2[c]	30,447[e]	.0	0
Transportation	241,378	..	285,504	..	54,944
Longshoremen	37,050[f]	+18.0	43,719	50.0	21,860
Sailors	14,109[f]	+15.0	16,225	25.0	4,056
Chauffeurs	49,185[f]	+25.0	61,481	20.0	12,296
Draymen and teamsters	28,785[f]	+10.0	31,664	20.0	6,333
Laborers, garage and roads	11,863[f]	+40.0	16,608	20.0	3,322
Telegraph operators	4,652[f]	+15.0	5,350	10.0	535
Telephone operators	21,419	+30.0	27,845	7.0	1,949
Street railroad (full-time)	33,559[g]	−1.6[c]	33,008[h]	1.4[c,i]	474[i,j]
" " (part-time)	5,531[g]	+32.6[c]	7,334[h]	11.5[c]	840[j]
Remainder of group	35,225	+20.0	42,270	10.0	4,227
Trade	392,397	..	497,393	..	32,863
Retail dealers	121,727	+25.0	152,159	2.0	3,043
Wholesale dealers, proprietors, officials	18,195	+10.0	20,015	.0	0
Clerks in stores	38,305	+30.0	46,797	9.0	4,212
Sales people	119,226	+30.0	154,994	9.0	13,949
Banking, insurance and real estate	39,769	+30.0	51,700	5.0	2,585
Deliverymen	11,974	+30.0	15,566	15.0	2,335
Laborers	18,259	+30.0	23,737	12.0	2,848
All others	24,942	+30.0	32,425	12.0	3,891
Public service	80,875[m]	..	119,260	..	1,730[i]
New York City Government	54,674[k]	+58.2[c]	86,509[k]	2.0[i]	1,730[i]
Remainder of group	26,201	+25.0	32,751	.0	0
Professional service	168,037	..	207,829	..	14,949
Actors	11,973	+30.0	15,565	15.0	2,335
Musicians	15,393	+30.0	20,011	20.0	4,002
Teachers	34,484	+30.0	44,829	5.0	2,241
All others	106,187	+20.0	127,424	5.0	6,371

(*See opposite page for foot notes*)

TABLE 13. ESTIMATED NUMBER UNEMPLOYED IN NEW YORK CITY, DECEMBER, 1930, BY OCCUPATIONAL GROUPS (*Continued*)

Occupational group	Gainfully employed			Estimated unemployment, December, 1930	
	Number, 1920 Census of Occupations	Estimated per cent change, 1920 to 1929	Estimated number, 1929	Per cent	Number
Domestic and personal service	306,290	..	378,059	..	49,768
Barbers, hairdressers.........	19,139	+50.0	28,709	10.0	2,871
Charwomen and cleaners......	7,111	+25.0	8,889	25.0	2,222
Elevator operators...........	10,159	+40.0	14,223	15.0	2,133
Laundry operators...........	9,942	+40.0	13,919	15.0	2,088
Laundry owners..............	2,494	+25.0	3,118	.0	0
Porters, not stores............	19,272	+15.0	22,163	20.0	4,433
Servants....................	114,782	+15.0	132,000	10.0	13,200
Waiters.....................	34,846	+40.0	48,784	25.0	12,196
All others...................	88,545	+20.0	106,254	10.0	10,625
Clerical occupations..............	382,414[m]	..	581,244	..	85,004
Gas and electricity...........	7,296[n]	+99.5	14,553[n]	.0	0
Remainder of group..........	375,118	+50.0	566,691	15.0	85,004
Agriculture, forestry and mining...	7,709	−50.0	3,855	10.0	386

[a] *Transit Record*, Board of Transportation of New York City. Figures for 1929 from January, 1930, issue. Figures for 1930 from January, 1931, issue.

[b] Estimated number based on United States Census of Manufactures for 1919.

[c] Number derived first and per cent computed therefrom.

[d] Estimated.

[e] New York State Public Service Commission for the First District, Annual Report, 1920, gives figures for 1920, p. 686. Figures for 1929 were received directly from the New York City Office of the Public Service Commission.

[f] Men only.

[g] New York State Public Service Commission for the First District, Annual Report, 1920, p. 409. Figures are as of June.

[h] New York State Transit Commission, Annual Report, 1929, p. 209. Figures are as of June.

[i] Increase in number employed.

[j] Computed by subtracting number employed in 1930 from those employed in 1929. Figures for 1930 were received directly from the New York City Office of the Public Service Commission.

[k] New York City Civil Service Commission, Annual Report, 1920, p. 12, and Annual Report, 1929, p. 14.

[m] 20,000 clerks were arbitrarily deducted from "clerical occupations" and added to "public service" to allow for the employees reported by the New York Civil Service Commission.

[n] New York State Public Service Commission for the First District, Annual Report, 1920, gives figures for 1920, p. 684. Figures for 1929 received directly from New York City Office of Public Service Commission.

stable than wage work. On the other hand, we must allow in this depression for a much greater tendency to economize on clerical help, in addition to the large reserve of clerical workers, for the reasons given above.[1]

The Public Employment Offices of the State Department of Labor report 935 clerical workers registered in November for each 100 jobs available.[2] More than eight out of nine clerks at present unemployed have no chance for employment with the demand remaining as it is. This is four times as bad as the situation in all industries combined. Even in November, 1929, there were 453 clerical workers for every 100 jobs.[3] With full allowance for the fact that the State Employment Office figures are not typical of the market for clerical work as a whole, the fact remains that we must allow for a larger percentage of unemployment than our current theories about clerical work might lead us to expect.

Agriculture and forestry

The number of workers engaged in agriculture and forestry in New York City is reduced one-half because so large a proportion of the land in Queens formerly used for market gardening has been taken for new housing developments. Some farming is still done in Queens and Staten Island, and a few greenhouse employees remain within the limits of the city.

All Occupations Combined

Given, therefore, the specific estimates for each of the several main occupational groups, we can arrive at a second estimate of unemployment in New York City by the exact opposite of the first method, that is, by proceeding from the parts instead of from the whole.

The second method gives us 572,572 unemployed people in December, 1930, among the 3,145,691 habitually gainfully employed in New York City. The proportion unemployed is 18.2 per cent.

SUPPLEMENTARY STUDIES

Trend of Employment in 1931

It would be quite impossible to make any estimate of the volume of employment during the coming months. The two factors are (1) seasonal changes, which recur with some regularity, and (2) the

---

[1] *Forbes Magazine* for March 15, 1931, reports that in this depression salaries have been reduced more than usual in place of wage rates. Article by B. C. Forbes, "Fact and Comment—Salaries Cut but Wages Stay up," p. 12.

[2] *Industrial Bulletin*, New York State Department of Labor, December, 1930, p. 80.

[3] *Ibid.*, December, 1929, p. 77.

possible improvement in general business, which is totally unpredictable. Both the normal seasonal movement and the tendency to a more pronounced seasonal decline in hard times make it absolutely certain that employment in January will be lower than that in December. The index of factory employment in New York City fell 4 per cent between December, 1930, and January, 1931.[1] We know also that retail stores make the largest cut in their forces of the entire year between December and January. In addition, many firms use the end of the year period to make adjustments in their personnel which they had hoped to avoid while a prospect of any early improvement seemed possible.

In February and March, the seasonal movement in New York City is upward. From April to July, there is a decline in the manufacturing industries but an increased pull from building and other outdoor industries. This seasonal upward movement will undoubtedly take place in 1931 and it alone is without significance as an indication of conditions in the following months, although it will be interpreted as evidence of basic improvement. Any evidence of cyclical recovery will be shown in the extent to which the index of factory employment for New York State as a whole shows a more than seasonal increase in March and April or a less than seasonal decline through the summer months. Since the New York State index of factory employment includes the principal metal industries, automobiles and building supplies, it is, if properly interpreted, an excellent guide to the trend of employment not only in manufacturing but in other industries.

The real test of the index of factory employment will come in August or September. If no rise is perceptible in August, if the increase in September and October is small, or if the line turns downward sharply in November, we may look for a large amount of unemployment next winter. The tests given here are not offered as a guide to the layman. The interpretation of these index figures cannot be done mechanically but is again a matter of weighing imponderables. It is true, however, that the trend can be seen ahead of the actual impact of unemployment and that it can be found in the slight variations of the seasonal movement of the index from its normal course.

On the whole, it is safe to say that probably the major reductions in employment have already taken place, that is, that the basic situation will get no worse. The principal ground for this hope is the fact that at last people in responsible places are taking a realistic

[1] The index for January was 73.7.

view of our business mistakes, and men who saw the error of the course we were pursuing in good times are now permitted to express their honest opinions. To say that the basic situation will not get worse is not, however, to say that all the secondary causes of dislocation have had their full effect. It is the secondary causes that affect the working man, and unless basic conditions really improve, rather than remaining stationary, we shall have as much unemployment or possibly more next winter than we have had this year. There are visible at present no reasons for assuming that the efforts to meet unemployment can be reduced within from three to twelve months, except for the temporary relief which always comes with outdoor work in summer.

Loss in Wages per Week

In order to arrive at an estimate of the loss in wages and salaries as a result of the unemployment of 1930, we have to know not only the number of unemployed but also the number of people on part time work and the level of wages for the unemployed when they were at work.

The Metropolitan Life Insurance survey for December, 1930, shows that in New York City 15 per cent of the policy holders were employed part time, in addition to the 23 per cent totally unemployed.[1] The percentage of unemployment among Metropolitan policy holders was five points higher than our estimate of unemployment for all those in gainful occupations. If we assume that part time for the total population differs from the Metropolitan part-time figures about the same as unemployment differs, we have to reduce the part-time figure to about 12 per cent instead of 15. The assumption that part time is less among the general population, as full-time unemployment was smaller for the general population than for policy holders, is open to question, for the reason that among large groups of people, especially in the higher reaches of the industrial scale, unemployment takes the form of part-time work rather than total unemployment. This is true, for instance, of nearly all professional workers like musicians, music teachers, dentists. It is true also of the small building contractors, who are practically wage-earners, and of many people whom the Census classes as "self-employed," from the Italian chestnut seller on the

---

[1] *New York Times*, January 25, 1931, Section I, p. 19, Article entitled "Idle Last Month Put at 5,000,000." Report to Senate by Col. Arthur Woods, based on survey made by Metropolitan Life Insurance Company among industrial policy holders.

Monthly Labor Review, U. S. Bureau of Labor Statistics, March, 1931, pp. 48–55.

street corner to the free lance reporter. New York has a high proportion of such workers. We have also reduced our estimate of technological unemployment in the analysis above on the theory that many of these people were able to get part-time work. For these reasons it is certain that an estimate of 12 per cent of part-time employment among the population usually in gainful occupations is on the side of conservatism.

The Buffalo study of unemployment in the general population referred to above shows part-time employment of 16.7 per cent in November, 1930, compared with full-time unemployment of 16.0 per cent for the same period. It is probably true that part-time unemployment is greater in Buffalo, where men tend to be attached not only to an industry but to a particular factory, than it is in New York City, where the factories are small and the alternative choice for jobs great, and the workers tend to be released completely rather than "laid off" to return to the same shop when business picks up. We have, therefore, 16.7 per cent as the upper limit to which part-time employment in New York City probably did not rise in November. We can tentatively assume, therefore, that part-time employment in New York City in December was somewhere between 12 per cent and 15 per cent of the population in gainful occupations, that is, from 378,000 to 472,000 people.

The Buffalo study indicates that of the 16.6 per cent of the working population that was employed part time; 6.9 per cent worked "two-thirds but less than full time," that is, four or five days, 6.5 per cent worked "one-half but less than two-thirds," that is, three or four days, and 3.2 per cent worked less than three days a week.[1] That is roughly equivalent to full-time unemployment of about 8 per cent. Taking the same rates—and again the "lay-off" by large firms tends to regularize conditions in Buffalo—the part-time employment in New York City is the equivalent of full-time unemployment for from 6 to 7 per cent of the population, or from 189,000 to 220,000 people. Here again, in all the elements of the estimate, the most conservative figure has been used. New York is a city of irregular employment in the best of times.

To arrive at a satisfactory estimate of average wages of those men and women who are unemployed, or working part time, is practically impossible. The index of factory employment for New York City gives average weekly earnings for all employed factory workers of $31.21 in November, 1930, and $32.32 in November,

[1] *Unemployment in Buffalo, November, 1930,* New York State Department of Labor, Special Bulletin No. 167, p. 11, Table 4.

1929.[1] We cannot assume that $32.32 was the usual average earnings of all the unemployed even in manufacturing, because the average earnings figure is sent up in part by dismissal of low-paid workers first and in part by the effects of technological unemployment. The men who were dismissed before the depression began were almost certainly not earning an average of $32.32 a week, and the men who were dismissed since also presumably fell below the average for all employed workers in manufacturing.

It is one of the curious phenomena of the New York State labor market index that average earnings often rise for the first few months after a depression begins because the lower-paid workers are let go. It is the highly paid designer and not the low-paid operator who is kept on. In the same way, part of the increase in average earnings over the last few years must be charged not to higher wages for the men at work but to the dismissal of low-paid workers to be replaced by machines.

We can again assume, therefore, that the "usual" wages of the men and women out of work in the manufacturing occupations would fall below $32.32 a week. How far can we use the average earnings in factories as an indicator of average earnings in all gainful employments? Here again we have the same phenomenon, that earnings in normal times outside of factory industries went higher and probably also lower than in factories, with no information whatever to indicate where the average would lie. It is the low-paid people who are dismissed, as it is the low-paid people who have the most part time.[2] For these reasons it is safe to assume that the average wage of the unemployed in all occupations would fall below the average wage of the employed in factories. On the other hand, it is true that in this depression we have had a large amount of dislocation in the higher-paid jobs, and in institutions like banks, commonly thought to be far removed from unemployment problems.

It is a common fallacy to assume that factory conditions are worse than employment and wage conditions in other industries. In New York City several important industries probably have wage levels much lower than factories but have escaped attention because they successfully resist efforts to compel them to report their wages and working conditions. Even a study of clerical wages and employment conditions in New York City would reveal conditions more

---

[1] *Industrial Bulletin*, New York State Department of Labor, December, 1930, p. 88.

[2] For a general discussion of part-time work in New York City, see *Employment and Earnings of Men and Women in New York State Factories, 1923–1925*, New York State Department of Labor, Special Bulletin No. 143, 1926.

like factory conditions than most people suspect. Such a study has long been urged by students of wages and labor conditions.

We have estimated that at least 18 per cent of those in gainful occupations were entirely without work in December, 1930, and that an additional 12 to 15 per cent were working part time, which is equivalent to full-time unemployment for at least 6 to 7 per cent of the total gainfully occupied population. We can assume that "lay-offs" in Buffalo slightly increased the proportion of those working four or five days for a factory which expected to take them back when conditions improved, whereas in New York City either those people were totally unemployed or moving from shop to shop doing casual work and, therefore, averaging less time per week than those "laid off." That gives us an equivalent of full-time unemployment in New York City of from 24 to 25 per cent of the population in gainful occupations. It adds something over 189,000 people to the minimum 572,000 totally unemployed according to Estimate II. The two figures together give the equivalent of full-time unemployment for over 750,000 people.

What can we take as a basis for estimating the wage loss of these 750,000? We know we cannot take a figure as high as the average weekly earnings of employed factory workers. The official figures can make no allowance for the "normally unemployed," so that average earnings, possible earnings, even in good times, must be noticeably lower than those reported for the men and women actually at work.

To get at possible earnings even for factory workers we must reduce the official average. To get at earnings for workers in non-factory industries we should probably find the average still lower. Making full allowance for the fact that a few highly paid people raise money averages very much, we still cannot assume an average income for workers in New York City in 1929 of $32.00 a week. We must assume also that the earnings of the people let go are lower than of those who are employed. Furthermore, the principal effect of technological inventions has almost certainly been to replace common labor in spite of the greater popular attention given to the elimination of old skilled trades. It is the men who were below the average and even below the median when they were employed who contribute the bulk of the unemployment.

It is true both that New York City has a large amount of unemployment in the higher scales of work and pay, and that this depression has probably led to more than the usual amount of reorganization by elimination of highly paid jobs. The whole effect of the displacement of the middle-aged is to replace people who have reached high levels because of years of service by young people whose salary level is much lower.

Because of these conflicting factors, no exact estimate of wages can be made, except to say that the average must fall below $32 a week and probably pretty well below. At an average loss in earned income of $32 a week for at least 750,000 unemployed people, we get an upper limit of $24,000,000 a week in lost earnings. If we reduce the normal average earnings of the unemployed to an estimate as low as $25 a week, we should still have a weekly wage loss of $18,750,000. This weekly wage loss is made up of accretions of losses from technological unemployment, seasonal and cyclical unemployment, losses due to lay-offs and part-time work, and finally the losses suffered by the normally unemployed. This is a social deficit of alarming proportions.

The Standard Statistics Company, in its estimate of unemployment, finds a decline of 20 per cent in earned incomes. This figure was published on October 15, 1930, and refers apparently to the situation in September, before the depression had reached anything like its present extent. An estimate of 25 per cent loss in earned incomes in New York in December is certainly not too high.

We can assume, therefore, that the people normally earning an income in New York City including office and professional people have had their earned incomes reduced an average of at least 25 per cent, or the equivalent of one week's income a month.

Metropolitan Life Insurance Study

A study of unemployment among industrial policy holders of the Metropolitan Life Insurance Company, just completed, gives for New York City 23.3 per cent wholly unemployed of the working members of families, 15 per cent employed part time, and 61.7 per cent employed full time. The census was taken the first week in December as of the week preceding the agent's visit and was limited to families of people carrying industrial policies.[1]

The survey bears out our assumption that complete separation from the job is commoner in New York City than part-time work.

The next question is how far industrial policy holders are representative of all New York City. Industrial insurance is characteristically the insurance of wage-earners. The Old Age Security Commission in New York State last year found that industrial policies were more widely held by the aged in New York City than in other

[1] See footnote, p. 44.

communities, largely because of the high cost of burial.[1] It is probably true also that in the extreme diversification of wealth in New York City there are relatively more poor and small income people than in other cities. On the other hand, the industrial policy holders exclude all professional people, most office workers, all those engaged in their own business except the very small tradesmen, most civil service employees. They exclude the more industrially stable elements of the population. The question is what proportion of the gainfully employed are in that more stable group, that is, how far the Metropolitan figure would be diminished if the sample had covered all the gainfully employed in New York City?

Unemployment in Philadelphia and Buffalo

An interesting comparison is afforded by taking the figures compiled by the Metropolitan Life Insurance Company in Philadelphia and Buffalo and comparing them with local surveys of unemployment in the general population in those cities.

An estimate of unemployment for Philadelphia in November, 1930, was prepared by the Industrial Research Department of the Wharton School of Commerce and Finance.[2] Their conclusions were that in November between 15 and 18 per cent of the city's gainfully employed population were looking for work and unable to find it.

TABLE 14. PER CENT UNEMPLOYED IN CERTAIN CITIES

City	Metropolitan study, industrial policy holders	Local studies, general population
Philadelphia	24.9 January, 1931	15–18 November, 1930
Buffalo	25.3 " "	16.0 " "
New York City	23.3 " "	18.2 December, 1930

In the Metropolitan Study, unemployment in New York City is slightly lower than that in Philadelphia and Buffalo. This difference in New York City, evident among policy holders, may not be true if professional and clerical workers and the semi-professional amusement groups are taken into consideration. At any rate, the important thing here is a comparison between the two sets of figures for

[1] *Report of New York State Commission on Old Age Security*, 1930, p. 206.

[2] *Employment Conditions in Philadelphia Area*, December 24, 1930, Industrial Research Department, Wharton School of Finance and Commerce, University of Pennsylvania, Philadelphia. Mimeographed report prepared for the Philadelphia Committee for Unemployment Relief and Philadelphia Permanent Committee on Employment.

each city. In Buffalo, the general population survey showed unemployment of 16.0 per cent in November, compared with 25.3 per cent for policy holders in January. In Philadelphia, the estimate, 15–18 per cent, averages 16.5 per cent, close to Buffalo, and compares also with 25 per cent for policy holders in January. The ratio, therefore, of general unemployment in November to unemployment among policy holders in January was practically the same in both Philadelphia and Buffalo. By using this ratio, we can again test the accuracy of our general estimate for New York City in December.

The percentage of unemployment for New York City in December was estimated at 18.2 per cent. It is necessary to change this tentatively to a November basis to make the comparison more useful. The New York City index of manufacturing employment declined from 79.9 in November to 77.0 in December. This is a decline of 2.9 points on the index, or 4 per cent of the employment in November. The percentage decline in employment for all industries was probably not as great from November to December, 1930, as the percentage decline in manufacturing, because of the Christmas trade. Assuming tentatively that the 4 per cent decline in manufacturing from November to December is the outside estimate of the difference between November and December for all industries, we should probably reduce the estimate of 18.2 per cent for December to about 15 per cent for November. At any rate, the ratio of the probable November figure for New York City general unemployment stands in about the same relation to the Metropolitan figure as the two series bear to each other in Philadelphia and in Buffalo.

Standard Statistics Company

The Standard Statistics Company of New York City made a careful estimate of unemployment in the United States for the fall of 1930. They used a very conservative estimate of the "normally unemployed," but even so they estimated 4,492,000 people unemployed for the United States as a whole, excluding agriculture, before the winter had set in.

Unemployment in 1914–15

In the industrial depression of 1914–15, two important studies were made of unemployment. The Bureau of Labor Statistics made a canvass of 104 carefully selected blocks in New York City, and the Metropolitan Life Insurance Company made a survey of its

TABLE 15. ESTIMATE OF UNEMPLOYMENT, UNITED STATES
Standard Statistics Company

	Number employed		Per cent change 1930 over 1929
	Year, 1929	Sept., 1930	
Railroads	1,687,000	1,564,300	−7.3
Manufacturing	8,451,400	7,040,000	−16.7
Construction	1,300,000	793,000	−39.0
Trade and service	12,522,000	11,104,500	−11.3
Water transportation	230,400	163,700	−28.9
Street railways	288,000	279,300	−3.0
Amusements	330,000	230,000	−30.3
Light and power	160,400	169,900	+5.9
Telephone and telegraph	426,400	426,400	..
Total[a]	26,377,000	22,635,000	−14.2

Summary
Number employed, 1929	26,377,000
Number employed, 1930	22,635,000
Reduction in number employed	3,742,000
Irreducible minimum of unemployment	750,000
Number of unemployed, 1930	4,492,000

From *Standard Trade and Securities*, Vol. 58, No. 7, October 15, 1930, Published by Standard Statistics Company.

[a] The total is greater than the sum of the items given.

policy holders similar to the one prepared in 1931.[1] The Metropolitan survey found unemployment among its policy holders of 18.0 per cent in January, 1915. The Bureau of Labor Statistics found unemployment of 16.2 per cent in the general population in February, 1915, a month of seasonal upturn. January, 1915, was the month in which the index number of employment in New York State factories reached its lowest point during the depression of 1914–15.

Both the Metropolitan and the Bureau of Labor Statistics made similar studies in September, 1915, to see how far employment had recovered from the low point.[2] Tables 16 and 17 show the findings of both investigations.

The Bureau of Labor Statistics survey also gives unemployment figures for the separate occupational groups of New York City which may be of interest in comparison with the estimates of unemployment in the separate industries made in this study.

[1] *Unemployment in New York City, New York*, U. S. Bureau of Labor Statistics, Bulletin No. 172.
Report of Mayor's Committee on Unemployment, New York City, 1916.
[2] *Unemployment in the United States*, U. S. Bureau of Labor Statistics, Bulletin No. 195.

The final estimate of unemployment for the entire city was 398,000[1] unemployed in February, 1915, according to the Bureau of Labor Statistics, and 442,000[2] in January, 1915, according to the Metropolitan Study, out of a gainfully employed population of 2,455,000.[1]

TABLE 16. PER CENT UNEMPLOYED, NEW YORK CITY, 1915
Canvass of 104 city blocks by U. S. Bureau of Labor Statistics[a]

Selected occupations	February, 1915[b]	September, 1915[c]
Building		
Bricklayers	32.5	14.7
Carpenters	25.9	7.2
Painters and paperhangers	43.9	7.8
Plasterers	37.1	14.0
Plumbers and steamfitters	23.1	11.9
Bakers	16.3	9.5
Bartenders	14.0	11.0
Chauffeurs	28.1	13.7
Cigar and tobacco workers	18.3	8.2
Laborers[d]	34.2	5.8
Longshoremen[d]	16.2	14.6
Machinists	13.1	4.7
Stonecutters	47.3	14.0
Stenographers and typists	5.2	3.9
Total[e]	16.2	6.7

[a] Survey of February, 1915, covered 130,138 men and 15,453 women in about 54,849 families.
Survey of September, 1915, covered 127,842 men and 37,094 women in about 56,539 families.
[b] *Unemployment in New York City, New York*, U. S. Bureau of Labor Statistics, Bulletin No. 172.
[c] *Unemployment in the United States*, U. S. Bureau of Labor Statistics, Bulletin No. 195.
[d] There is probably some confusion in reporting between laborers and longshoremen.
[e] Total includes more items than those given above.

TABLE 17. ESTIMATED UNEMPLOYMENT IN NEW YORK CITY, 1915
Based on a survey of Metropolitan Life Insurance Company Policy Holders

Month and year	Men	Women	Total	Per cent of policy holders unemployed
January, 1915	351,249	90,751	442,000	18.0
September, 1915	177,417	46,877	224,294	9.1

From *Unemployment in the United States*, U. S. Bureau of Labor Statistics, Bulletin No. 195, p. 108.

[1] *Unemployment in New York City, New York*, U. S. Bureau of Labor Statistics, Bulletin No. 172, p. 8.
[2] *Ibid.*, p. 15. Computed as 18 per cent of 2,455,000.

Table 18. Per Cent Change in Employment from December, 1913, to December, 1914

Reports from employers

Occupational group	Per cent change, Dec., 1913 to Dec., 1914
Steam railroads	−3.2
Electric railroads	+12.2
Transfer and drayage	−27.1
Water transportation	−11.1
Electric light and power	−4.3
Gas	+1.9
Telephone and telegraph	+0.7

From *Report of Mayor's Committee on Unemployment*, New York City, 1916, p. 11.

Unemployment in 1921

It is not possible to arrive at an exact estimate of the amount of unemployment in 1921. The principal source of information, the index of factory employment in New York State, is continuous from June, 1914, to date. It gives us a measure of the decline in employment from the high point of 1920 to the low point of 1921 in manufacturing in terms of index numbers, which can be changed to an estimate of unemployment only with certain definite assumptions. The high point in the index series for 1920 was 127.6 in March, the month in which the turn from inflation to depression first appeared. The low point of employment came in August of 1921 with an index number of 89.7. This means a decline of 37.9 points, or 30 per cent. The corresponding decline between the high point of 1929 and the low point of 1930 for New York State was about 23 per cent.[1]

For several important reasons, we cannot assume from these figures that the depression of 1921 was more severe than that of 1930. Most important is the fact that the depression of 1930 came after several years of diminishing employment, so-called technological unemployment. Miss Clinch Calkins' book, "Some Folks Won't Work," is a study of unemployment completed before the depression of 1930 began, and based, therefore, entirely on unemployment which existed in the midst of our last boom. That means that we must add to the decline in employment shown by employers' reports a larger amount for "normal unemployment" and for technological unemployment than it was necessary to add in 1921, a depression following years in which many families had had more workers in gainful occupations as a result of the war than formerly had been so employed.

[1] *Industrial Bulletin*, New York State Department of Labor.

In the second place, as a result of the diminished employment in our recent period of prosperity, the workers entered upon this depression with very much less in the way of savings than they had in 1920. It is well known that the second year of a depression is much worse than the first, even if there is no increase in the volume of unemployment. The first reserves of the worker have been used up and his family, his friends, and his savings can no longer be relied upon. Medical and dental work have been postponed and clothes have not been replaced. In an important sense, the depression of 1930 began with what was socially a second year of unemployment. That is, many workers who had had to draw upon their normal reserves even during the good years were not equipped to carry themselves through a year of general unemployment as well as if 1929 had been as prosperous for the worker as we used to say it was.

In the third place, we may raise the question whether in 1921 the depression may not have affected the manufacturing industries relatively more than other industries, whereas in 1930 manufacturing may have been spared some of the worst effects and other industries received some of the dislocation. This is a question on which experts disagree. We have been confident until recently that there was comparatively little disturbance in the basic structure of manufacturing, whereas we know there was a very serious disturbance in 1921. Recently we have come to see that manufacturing was more subtly affected by our speculative disease than we had realized. Even so, it seems to us that there was truth in the contention that manufacturing was more immediately and violently affected, compared with other industries, in 1921 than it was in 1930. It may take manufacturing much longer to recover than we had expected because of this subtle destruction of some of its healthy tissue, but there is evidence enough that this depression has affected every phase of industry and commerce, as much at least as any depression since 1893.

It is not possible to compare the decline in manufacturing in 1921 with that in 1914 by means of the index series of factory employment in New York State, because the series begins in June, 1914, a period some time after the peak of employment had been passed. The total decline shown by the index numbers goes from 101.8 in June, 1914, to 93.3 in January, 1915. We have no means, however, of knowing how much higher the top level of employment of 1914 would have been than the figures given in the records for June. The year 1914 was one in which unemployment was slowly increasing, even before the European War brought about a sudden decline in the second half of the year. Recovery, of course, was much quicker in 1915 than in 1921 because of the influence of European war contracts.

Method

The information available about unemployment in New York City varies from an exact count of employees in corporations subject to official bodies like the Public Service Commission to vague and contradictory estimates for industries subject to no public supervision whatever. The method has been to get exact counts where they were available, sample figures where they could be had, and estimates or illuminating figures from related series, either of employment in other states or other items than employment, where that was the best available information.

In the use of estimates in this report, especially in connection with Estimate II, several things have been kept in mind. In the absence of specific numerical information about various industries, we have tried to arrive at evidences of tendency and proportions. If we do not know exact figures for the increase or decrease in a particular industry, we know something qualitative to show its similarity to or dissimilarity with other industries. By putting this information together with a careful sense of the relation of the various parts to each other and to the whole, it is possible to arrive at a reliable kind of estimate which is dependent in part on quantitative data, in part upon qualitative knowledge of the industrial situation as a whole, and on a sense of proportion in putting these items of information together. In other words, the justification for this method is not so much arithmetical as geometric or structural.

This leads to a further element of safety. Separate items were not estimated only in relation to available information about one industry or one occupation, but were considered always as part of a total flow of industry. That means that they were not a separate series of estimates, any one of which could be raised or lowered without reference to others, but rather they were all part of a structure, the separate elements of which stood or fell together.

The method used in estimating employment in 1929 was virtually the same as the method used in estimating unemployment in 1930. As a result of this method of getting at employment in 1929 by putting together the available information about separate items, the total estimate for the gainfully employed in New York City came out at 3,145,691. An estimate made by the opposite method of applying the proportion of gainfully employed in 1920 to the population for 1930 gave us a gainfully employed population of 3,163,701, a very small difference considering the difference in method. Again, the estimate of the number of unemployed, derived from the United States Census of the Unemployed taken April 1, 1930, gives us a figure close to the estimate derived from the method of accumulating evidence about separate industries.

Finally, in all the estimates used in the foregoing study, minimum figures were taken wherever possible. The results, therefore, are as conservative as possible.

Institute of Public & Social Administration
40 E. Ferry St.
Detroit, : Michigan

Printed by Amazon Italia Logistica S.r.l.
Torrazza Piemonte (TO), Italy